THE
EASY APPETIZER
COOKBOOK

THE EASY APPETIZER COOKBOOK

NO-FUSS RECIPES FOR ANY OCCASION

SARAH WALKER CARON

Photography by Cayla Zahoran

ROCKRIDGE
PRESS

Interior and Cover Designer: Michael Patti
Art Producer: Sara Feinstein
Editor: Barbara J. Isenberg
Production Editor: Edgar Doolan
Production Manager: Holly Haydash
Photography: © 2019 Cayla Zahoran
Food Styling: Jennifer Ophir

ISBN: Print 978-1-64152-946-4
eBook 978-1-64152-947-1

For my children's mouths . . . and their
bellies, too, I suppose.
Will and Paige, may you smile bright
and remember always.

CONTENTS

Introduction viii

CHAPTER ONE
PARTY PLANNING 101

CHAPTER TWO
LIGHT SNACKS

Citrus-Garlic Marinated Olives 16

Sweet and Spicy Roasted Nuts 17

Gourmet Parmesan-Herb Popcorn 18

Rosemary-Thyme Parmesan Crisps 20

Chef's Salad Skewers 22

Balsamic-Drizzled Fruit and
Cheese Bites 23

Marinated Mozzarella with
Sun-Dried Tomatoes 24

Marinated Feta with Rosemary
and Orange 25

Greek Salad–Inspired Cucumber Bites 26

Roasted Vegetable Kabobs 27

CHAPTER THREE
DIPS & SPREADS

Chunky Guacamole 30

Fresh Tomato Salsa 31

Avocado, Mango, and Pineapple Salsa 32

Fresh Basil Whipped Feta Dip 33

Caramelized Shallot and Pine Nut
Hummus 34

Sun-Dried Tomato–Garlic White Bean Dip 35

Spicy Black Bean Dip 36

Homemade Onion Dip 38

Spinach Artichoke Dip 39

Quick and Easy Raspberry
Refrigerator Jam 40

CHAPTER FOUR
FINGER FOODS

Rosemary-Garlic Whipped Ricotta Crostini
with Prosciutto 44

Tomato Caprese Bruschetta 45

Miniature Baking Soda Biscuits
for a Crowd 46

Crispy Oven-Roasted Party Wings 48

Stuffed Mini Sweet Peppers with Whipped Feta 50

Deviled Eggs, Three Ways 51

Bacon-Wrapped Asparagus 52

Mediterranean Marinated Chicken Skewers 53

Barbecue Chicken-Pineapple Bites 54

Chicken Caesar Salad Cups 55

How to Assemble a Cheese Board 56

CHAPTER FIVE

SAVORY PLATES

Peanut Chicken Endive Bites 60

California Turkey Burger Sliders 62

Honey, Ham, and Brie Party Sandwiches 63

Hummus Veggie Pinwheels 64

Classic Party Meatballs 65

Sheet Pan Party Pizza 66

Veggie Wontons 68

Cheese-Stuffed Chicken Meatballs Marinara 70

Mini Taco Bites 72

Buffalo Chicken Wraps with Blue Cheese 73

CHAPTER SIX

FANCY BITES

Raspberry Baked Brie en Croute 76

Caramelized Onion, Mushroom, and Gouda Pinwheels 77

Fig, Gorgonzola, and Pear Tartlets 78

Polenta with Lemony Tomato Bruschetta 79

Mini Quiche Lorraine 80

Shrimp Satay with Peanut Dipping Sauce 82

Crab-Stuffed Mushrooms 84

Garlic-Ginger Portobello Mushrooms 86

Salmon Fritters 88

Crispy Garlic Butter Smashed Potatoes 89

CHAPTER SEVEN

SOMETHING SWEET

Raspberry-Watermelon Smoothie Shooters 92

Fruit Skewers with Creamy Marshmallow Dip 93

Double-Chocolate Brownie Bites 94

Salted Peanut Butter Cookies 96

Cinnamon Swirl Mini Cupcakes 98

Chocolate Chip Mini Cheesecakes 100

Mini Apple Pies with Crumb Topping 102

Glazed Strawberry Tartlets 104

S'mores Tarts 105

Cinnamon Sugar Pinwheels 106

The Dirty Dozen™ and the Clean Fifteen™ 107

Measurement Conversions 108

Index 109

INTRODUCTION

LINGERING AROUND THE cool granite of my kitchen island, the laughter reverberates off the walls. Wine flows freely. Hands extend to the cheese board, selecting a sliver of aged Gouda, a seedy cracker, maybe a slice of sausage. There's a river of fancy local salami and a sea of prosciutto inviting edible exploration. A jar of marmalade makes a tinkling sound as the spoon hits the rim, on its way to be dolloped on a slice of bread topped with Fromager d'Affinois.

It's comforting—these sounds, this food, this experience. It's relaxed and free—the opposite of stressful.

This story repeats itself—when my family visits for Thanksgiving, when my colleagues gather for a dinner, when my cookbook club meets—and each time, it leaves me craving more. Gathering with people of shared interests and experiences is a soul-filling experience. I count my blessings and consider how soon we can do it again.

Hosting cocktail and dinner parties is something I've been drawn to for as long as I can remember. In college, it felt like the activity of a grown-up, something that drew a line in the sand between my childhood and adulthood. As a recent graduate, it felt like the thing we should be doing.

But now, nearly two decades later, it's a calling, something my spirit craves. Every bit of the planning and preparation for the party is a joy. It's piecing together a puzzle of people, flavors, and sips to form a complete picture of companionship and care and kindness. I want to have people over again and again and again, enjoying each other's company.

It wasn't always this way. In my early twenties, when it felt like something we should be doing, the pressures of having guests over seemed to bubble up and explode—if only in my head. I was anxious about menus and having enough food and drinks. I felt unprepared—a fraud in my own kitchen, unsure and unready. I felt like a kid playing dress-up.

I wasn't the Zen Super Bowl host my parents' friends were when they welcomed dozens of people into their home for a Sunday night every year. I wasn't able to harness the help of everyone around the way my friend's mother did when she hosted a bridal shower while we vacationed at Cape May one summer. And I definitely wasn't the force of nature my cousin Grace Louise was when our massive extended family would descend on her Cape Cod home every summer for a busy, noisy, exuberant family reunion.

At some point, though, I realized I didn't need to be any of those people. Wonderful memories of those parties remind me that having friends and family over is a wonderful soul-filling thing, but they needn't come with pressures and expectations. As hostesses, we each need to forge our own path and find our own way of doing things. For me, that's having an organized system for planning ahead, forgiving myself for forgetting things (Napkins? Meh, let's use these handy paper towels instead), and creating a menu I enjoy making and guests enjoy eating.

My spread doesn't need to span the length of my dining room table, as my parents' friends' did, or, especially, the length of a barn as Grace Louise's did. I don't need the help of a dozen people to pull things together as my friend's mom did.

Adding an olive tray to the table isn't cheating; it's offering a low-stress addition to the spread. Same with veggie trays and baguettes. Choosing a few easy, flavorful recipes to make is part of the fun. Ultimately, I want to host a welcoming party that's soundtracked with the jingle of laughter and soft sounds of food being enjoyed. I want my guests to leave with smiles on their faces.

Through this book on easy appetizers, I hope I can inspire you, too. Hosting friends for appetizers doesn't have to be a stressful experience. And the more you do it, the more comfortable you'll be with it. Drop the expectations of parties past—you don't need to live up to what another host did. Instead, create a fun, stress-less spread to enjoy with friends. And then really enjoy it. Because that's what's important.

CHAPTER ONE

PARTY PLANNING 101

WHEN FRIENDS and family gather around the kitchen island or congregate in the living room for a gathering, laughter and joy and merriment happen. If you aren't having people over now, it's time to start doing so. You won't regret it.

But hosting fun, stress-free gatherings requires planning and preparation. In this chapter, you'll learn how to create a good, doable, easy menu and execute it. You'll also learn how to plan your beverages, what serving pieces (especially ones that can do double duty!) you need, and discover some ready-to-go menu ideas.

Ready? Let's get planning!

<< LEFT: RASPBERRY BAKED BRIE EN CROUTE (PAGE 76)

CHOOSING A MENU

THE DATE IS SET, the guests are invited, and you're psyched for a good time. Now comes the work: planning the food to serve. Feeding your guests well is important. You want people to feel welcome in your home and enjoy being there—and choosing a good menu can help.

First, define your party for yourself. Is it a casual gathering or more formal? Will your guests gather in your kitchen or do you plan to have them mingling throughout your living and dining areas? Maybe on the porch? Or perhaps they'll sit, as they would for a sports-viewing party. Also, how many guests do you anticipate? Will there be dinner after appetizers, or is this a strictly appetizers-only gathering?

Write those details down. They'll be important to remember throughout the planning process. Writing them down ensures they remain at the forefront of your mind.

From there, creating the menu is part art and part science. The art comes in selecting foods with complementary flavors. They don't have to be the same flavors—for instance, if you have one lemony dish, they shouldn't all be lemony—but you want to ensure that everything can be enjoyed together. On the science end, it comes down to cooking times and processes. You don't want dishes that have to be cooked in the same way at the same time. Instead, mix it up with make-ahead options and ones that can be prepared quickly and easily just before serving. You want guests to enjoy what you serve.

How do you do all that? These tips will help.

CELEBRATE THE CONTRASTS

As the saying goes, opposites attract. So, as you plan your menu, pair heavier foods like meatballs with lighter ones like salad skewers. Crispy party wings pair well with creamier foods like chunky guacamole. Avoid, for instance, serving four dips together. It's too much of a good thing.

Ultimately, you are aiming for variety in taste, texture, mouthfeel, and heaviness. Variety in the temperature of food is good, too. So, cool creamy Marinated

Feta with Rosemary and Orange (page 25) might be perfect served with warm and crispy Bacon-Wrapped Asparagus (page 52).

TIMING MATTERS

Position your party for success by remembering to factor in timing as you choose recipes. For the most stress-free shindig, aim primarily for make-ahead foods. Dishes with last-minute prep should be kept to a minimum.

Really, though, don't choose a menu of recipes that all have to be cooked at once on the day of the party. It's a recipe for a stressful disaster.

Also, the time of day you choose to host your party matters as well. Why? Because it will determine how much food you need. Afternoon parties, for instance, tend to bring out lighter appetites so you won't need as much food. Meanwhile, evening parties draw hungry guests. See By the Numbers (page 4) for more on this.

KITCHEN SPACE AND SCHEDULING

How much space do you have to work with? If you're in a mini kitchen—complete with a mini refrigerator, which is common in some city dwellings—you'll want to tailor your menu to the space you have. For instance, meatballs might be a good option for serving because they can be made on the day of the party and stored in a slow cooker until you're ready to serve. On the other hand, taco bites might be better skipped as they need a lot of toppings—which take up space.

Likewise, if you want to have a few hot appetizers, make sure you aren't planning more than your oven can handle. Choose either Honey, Ham, and Brie Party Sandwiches (page 63) or Raspberry Baked Brie en Croute (page 76), for instance, but not both.

Write out your cooking schedule to help with your planning and organization. You'll want to note several things:

- **What's on the menu**—Create a full list of what you're serving, including recipes and any accompaniments like crackers or fruit plates.

- **Note what can be made ahead**—Use an asterisk or other mark to identify the recipes that can be made ahead of time and stored until ready to serve.

- **Note what must be made fresh**—Put a dash or other mark to identify the recipes that must be made at the last minute. Include the total time needed to make these recipes.

- **Plan when to cook make-ahead recipes**—If they can be made the day before, do it, or plan another cooking time that works for you.

- **Create a day-of-party schedule**—Working backward from the time the party starts, create a schedule for when dishes need to be prepared and cooked, as well as when you'll do associated tasks like plating other appetizers or setting the table.

Once that's done, make a shopping list. Using your menu, go through each item and jot down what you need to purchase. Don't forget non-food items, like napkins and paper plates, if you need them.

I am a big proponent of using paper plates for casual parties since they make cleanup so much easier. Still, some fancier parties do call for real plates. Do what works for you and your party.

BY THE NUMBERS

When will you hold your party? This is an important element to consider when deciding how much food you'll need to serve. Timing is, ultimately, everything. Afternoon parties, for instance, require less food. People tend to be less hungry at this time, after lunch but before dinner. Evening parties, on the other hand, require more food. But how much food is that?

Good question. It can be tricky to know, can't it? But armed with a little knowledge, it gets easier. This simple formula will help ensure you have the right amount of food to feed your hungry guests.

AFTERNOON GET-TOGETHERS (1 TO 2 HOURS)

Having friends over for book club? Drinks on the deck? These shorter afternoon parties require less food because folks are between meals. Plan on 4 or 5 appetizer pieces per guest. A good mix of appetizers for this type of party is 2 or 3 appetizers. Aim for lighter appetizers such as those in chapter 2, Light Snacks, and chapter 4, Finger Foods. The Peanut Chicken Endive Bites (page 60) are also good for this.

COCKTAIL HOUR BEFORE DINNER (1 TO 2 HOURS)

When you are hosting a dinner party but don't want to dive right into dinner, cocktails and appetizers can be just the thing. Like afternoon parties, these require less food as guests are anticipating dinner later. But you will need a little more food than you would for an afternoon party since guests tend to be hungrier in the evening. Plan on 5 to 7 appetizer pieces per guest. You'll want to prepare 3 to 5 appetizers. For cocktail hour, recipes in chapter 4, Finger Foods, are ideal. A recipe from chapter 3, Dips & Spreads, can also round out the offering. Or, instead of multiple appetizers, create a big cheese board with 3 or 4 types of cheese and 1 or 2 types of meat, crackers, bread, and other accompaniments (see page 56).

LONGER COCKTAIL PARTY BEFORE DINNER (2 TO 3 HOURS)

Bigger affairs—such as cocktail parties at events, conferences, and post-wedding, pre-dinner festivities—require more food, and especially more filling food. That way, the guests won't get hungry and testy. If your cocktail party will go on for hours, you'll need more food to keep guests satiated. Plan on 7 to 10 pieces per person and a mix of 5 or 6 appetizers. Recipes from chapter 4, Finger Foods, and chapter 6, Fancy Bites, with 1 or 2 recipes from chapter 5, Savory Plates, would be good for this type of appetizer spread.

COCKTAIL PARTY WITHOUT DINNER (3 TO 4 HOURS)

Some of my favorite parties don't involve an actual dinner at all. They're longer, so you can really have some fun, but they are casual, appetizer-filled parties. If your event is all appetizers and no dinner, then, like a longer cocktail party, you'll need more appetizers. Plan on 8 to 12 pieces per person and a mix of 6 or 7 appetizers. For this style of party, choose a few recipes from chapter 5, Savory Plates, and mix it up with ones from chapter 6, Fancy Bites; chapter 4, Finger Foods; chapter 3, Dips & Spreads; and chapter 2, Light Snacks.

PANTRY AND FREEZER STAPLES

A well-stocked pantry and freezer make cooking for any occasion quick and easy. But, particularly when it comes to appetizers, having the right items on hand can make last-minute prep a breeze—whether you have guests on the way or need a dish to take with you to a party.

But what should you keep on hand? The following pantry and freezer staples are a good place to start.

- **Frozen puff pastry:** Good for both appetizers and desserts (plus cinnamon rolls, in a pinch), puff pastry is frozen and simply needs to be defrosted before using. That takes about 45 minutes. Keep at least one box in the freezer at all times!

- **Olives:** When jarred (and canned!) olives go on sale, pick up a few to keep in the pantry. They last a long time and are an excellent finger food to lay out when unexpected guests arrive. You can also marinate them—try my Citrus-Garlic Marinated Olives (page 16)—toss them in salads, and cook with them.

- **Crackers:** Cheese, dip, charcuterie . . . all are delightful with crackers, another pantry staple. Keep at least one unopened box in the pantry at all times to pull out. As for variety, choose one you love.

- **Nuts:** A canister or jar of nuts goes a long way. Perfect for nibbling with beer or setting out in bowls while dinner cooks, this is a simple and great finger food. Mixed nuts can feel more elegant, but everyone loves almonds, don't they?

- **Canned beans:** Whether you favor white beans, crave black beans, or adore chickpeas (garbanzo beans), this pantry staple is essential for last-minute dips and salads.

- **Popcorn kernels:** It's so easy to pop popcorn on the stove and in the microwave (see Gourmet Parmesan-Herb Popcorn, page 18, for directions!). And then you can dress it up for a fun, flavorful snack.

- **Roasted red peppers:** From a quick and easy bruschetta to a tasty deviled egg topping, these peppers have so many uses in the kitchen. They can also dress up a cheese plate.

- **Extra-virgin olive oil:** This is a staple for all things kitchen life. Use it to dress salads, drizzle on vegetables before roasting, and to fry eggs. Or season some with some good salt and herbs and drip crusty bread into it.

- **Balsamic glaze:** Likewise, this is a kitchen staple with so many uses. It's great on salads, especially appealing on sliced tomatoes, and perfect mixed with that extra-virgin olive oil for a dipping sauce. Or drizzle it on pizza, fruit, potatoes, or just about anything for a flavor boost.

TOOLS WORTH HAVING

In my kitchen, I prefer to have only the tools we use regularly. For that reason, I have a variety of shredders and graters in various sizes as I hand-shred all our cheeses, as well as carrots for salads. Likewise, I have a stash of lightweight, easy-to-use metal mixing bowls that are perfect for holding ingredients while I prep them for cooking, as well as for mixing batters and fillings.

In addition to these, I have a few tools that don't take up a lot of space but do make food prep easier and faster:

- **Mini food processor**—Inexpensive and compact, a mini food processor is a must for making dips and spreads. With a wider and flatter blade than a blender, it's ideally suited for finely chopping ingredients. Plus, you can use it to make pesto and other sauces. Mine is a 3-cup version, but 4-cup versions are available.

- **Hand-held juicer**—You've probably seen this tool, often brightly colored. You place half a lemon or lime inside, squeeze the sides together, and juice comes out of the little holes on one side. It's so useful when squeezing lime juice for guacamole or lemon juice for sauces.

- **Good, sharp knives**—These are not optional. Sharp knives don't just make kitchen work go smoother and faster, they are safer, too. How does that work? With dull knives, you have to work harder to cut, chop, and mince, and that often leads to accidents. So, invest in some good, sharp knives for your kitchen. A chef's knife, paring knife, and Santoku knife for mincing will get you started.

- **Avocado tool**—I love giving this tool as a gift because it's so useful. With this tool, you can cut open, pit, peel, and slice an avocado. So easy! And so, so worth it.

- **Sheet pan**—Originally, I bought a full-size sheet pan for cooking for events. But when I realized how easy it is to bake two dozen cookies at once, I started using this for everything. It makes quick work of big baking jobs.

SERVING ESSENTIALS

Arranging food for serving and setting it out is half the fun of hosting parties. As you prepare and plate food, keep an eye on the aesthetics. For some foods, like hummus and black bean dip, a little garnish goes a long way in terms of making a great tasting food look great, too. Also, be sure to make your dishes accessible. The tower of baby carrots might be pretty, but if your guests are afraid to eat one for fear of having them all crash down like a house of cards, then it's probably not a good idea to serve them that way.

Also, you don't need a cupboard full of items you use once a year. The key to choosing serving pieces is to select ones that can double for everyday use. After all, if you have it, why not use it?

The following serving essentials are useful items that can do double duty for parties and everyday use. No waste here!

- **Appetizer plates:** Are these really essential? I think so. Small plates are easy to store and make a more elegant presentation at cocktail parties. On an everyday basis though, these are great for snacks, light breakfasts, and for appetizers for dinner. I have two sets in my cupboard that get used regularly—and, together, they are perfect for parties.

- **Large, nice wood cutting board:** This is great for everyday food prep. But it's also an essential serving tool for parties. I use mine for cheese boards, fruit boards, and serving meat.

- **Pedestal stand/cake stand:** This might seem like a single-use item, but really, it has potential for regular usage—particularly if you get one with a cover. Use it for adding height to your appetizer spread during parties or for holding bite-size desserts. For everyday use, use it for Bundt cakes, coffee cakes, bread, and as a fancy place to keep countertop lemons.

- **Platters:** Platters are essential for serving appetizers at cocktail parties. Choose a few with different shapes and sizes to keep on hand, such as a round, an oval, and an oblong or square one. They are also great for family-style dinners and holidays.

- **Serving spoons:** I have five of these in my silverware drawer and have never hosted a party where they didn't all get used. And, on any given week, we use these to dish up salad, serve sauces, and share fruit cups. Tablespoons are also great to have on hand for dips.

- **Small, medium, and large serving bowls:** These are great for holding chips, popcorn, and nuts at parties. But they also work for pastas, salads, dips, and more. Choose ones that are dishwasher safe and you'll use them all the time. Bonus points if the bowls you select nest inside each other (so much easier for storing!).

- **Toothpicks:** From skewering little bites to setting out with meatballs, these are excellent to have on hand for parties. But did you know that toothpicks have practical everyday uses, too? Use them as cake testers, to hold together unruly sandwiches and wraps, or to feel fancy while eating olive bar olives from the plastic container.

Typically, when I host parties, I let beautifully arranged food be the decoration. But if you like flowers, for instance, keep a few vases on hand. Votive candles or tapers with nice candleholders can add to the ambience, if you are so inclined. A full set of wine glasses is excellent if you enjoy wine with your appetizers. Stemless tumblers can be a great alternative and feel a little less awkward when drinking sparkling juice instead of wine.

DRINK PAIRINGS

Beverages are an important component of any gathering. From backyard parties to fancier affairs, spend time considering which drinks to have on hand—and how much to have.

First, as with the food, consider the timing and style of the gathering you're hosting. For an afternoon get-together, you may want to offer all nonalcoholic drinks, such as lemonade, iced tea, and water.

For evening parties, you may want to offer wine, beer, or even a signature cocktail.

But what should be served with what? I have good news: Appetizers tend to be very flexible when it comes to pairings. Truly, the best drink pairing is the one you like. When planning parties, plan to have a variety of drinks on hand, including nonalcoholic options. Not everyone wants to or can drink alcohol.

Drinks that pair well with light appetizers: cider (alcoholic), infused water (water with flavor enhancers, such as herbs or sliced strawberries, lemons, oranges, or cucumbers), seltzer, sparkling lemonade, juice, and white wine
Drinks that pair well with heavier appetizers: beer, juice, red wine, and soda
Universally good drinks to offer: beer, iced tea, lemonade/sparkling lemonade, red and white wine, water

How much do you need?

- **For wine:** Plan to have 1 bottle per every 4 guests for every hour of the party, and mix it up between red and white, as desired.

- **For beer and cider:** Plan to have 1 can/bottle per guest per hour of the party.

- **For spirits:** Plan to have enough to make each guest 2 cocktails. Having a signature cocktail makes choosing spirit varieties easier.

- **For nonalcoholic drinks:** Plan on about 2 liters per 4 guests per hour of the party.

Another way to look at it is to consider what drinks you want to offer. If you just want wine and nonalcoholic options, which is my preference, have 50 percent wine and 50 percent nonalcoholic drinks. If offering wine, beer/cider, and nonalcoholic options, plan on 50 percent wine, 30 percent beer/cider, and 20 percent nonalcoholic choices.

MENU IDEAS

THE FOLLOWING MENU ideas combine recipes in this cookbook for different gatherings as a guide for choosing the optimal menu. Note the estimated party time in each menu. Start with these suggestions for inspiration and change, switch, and arrange your menu however you and your guests will love it.

SUMMER DRINKS
`(1 TO 2 HOURS)`

Citrus-Garlic Marinated Olives 16

Marinated Mozzarella with Sun-Dried Tomatoes 24

Roasted Vegetable Kabobs 27

POOL PARTY
`(3 TO 4 HOURS)`

Balsamic-Drizzled Fruit and Cheese Bites 23

Fresh Basil Whipped Feta Dip with veggies and crackers 33

Mediterranean Marinated Chicken Skewers 53

Sheet Pan Party Pizza 66

Polenta with Lemony Tomato Bruschetta 79

AWARDS SHOW VIEWING PARTY
`(3 TO 4 HOURS)`

Gourmet Parmesan-Herb Popcorn 18

Greek Salad–Inspired Cucumber Bites 26

Spinach Artichoke Dip 39

Bacon-Wrapped Asparagus 52

Honey, Ham, and Brie Party Sandwiches 63

Caramelized Onion, Mushroom, and Gouda Pinwheels 77

GAME DAY PARTY

(3 TO 4 HOURS)

Sweet and Spicy
Roasted Nuts 17

Chef's Salad Skewers 22

Chunky Guacamole 30

Fresh Tomato Salsa 31

Crispy Oven-Roasted Party
Wings 48

Mini Taco Bites 72

PRE-EVENT DRINKS

(ABOUT 1 HOUR)

Rosemary-Thyme Parmesan
Crisps 20

Sun-Dried Tomato–Garlic
White Bean Dip 35

Peanut Chicken Endive
Bites 60

A VEGAN FEAST

(3 TO 4 HOURS)

Citrus-Garlic Marinated
Olives 16

Roasted Vegetable
Kabobs 27

Caramelized Shallot
and Pine Nut Hummus 34

Hummus Veggie
Pinwheels 64

Veggie Wontons 68

Polenta with Lemony
Tomato Bruschetta 79

HOLIDAY PARTY

(3 TO 4 HOURS)

Marinated Feta with
Rosemary and Orange 25

Quick and Easy Raspberry
Refrigerator Jam 40

Miniature Baking Soda
Biscuits for a Crowd 46

Stuffed Mini Sweet Peppers
with Whipped Feta 50

Deviled Eggs, Three Ways 51

Classic Party Meatballs 65

Crab-Stuffed
Mushrooms 84

NEW YEAR'S CELEBRATION

(4 TO 5 HOURS)

Peanut Chicken Endive
Bites 60

Cheese-Stuffed Chicken
Meatballs Marinara 70

Raspberry Baked
Brie en Croute 76

Fig, Gorgonzola, and Pear
Tartlets 78

Shrimp Satay with Peanut
Dipping Sauce 82

Crispy Garlic Butter
Smashed Potatoes 89

FALL COCKTAILS

(1 TO 2 HOURS)

Citrus-Garlic Marinated
Olives 16

Rosemary-Thyme
Parmesan Crisps 20

Spicy Black Bean Dip 36

Tomato Caprese
Bruschetta 45

CHAPTER TWO

LIGHT SNACKS

FROM DRINKS on the patio to little bites served while dinner cooks, light snacks are perfect for munching. Make one or a few of these recipes and have them ready for guests to enjoy. All recipes in this chapter can be made ahead, which makes planning and serving a breeze.

<< LEFT: CITRUS-GARLIC MARINATED OLIVES (PAGE 16)

CITRUS-GARLIC MARINATED OLIVES

SERVES 8 PREP TIME: 10 MINUTES, PLUS 30 MINUTES TO MARINATE

5 INGREDIENTS | DAIRY-FREE | GLUTEN-FREE | GOOD FOR LEFTOVERS | MAKE AHEAD | NUT-FREE | ONE POT | VEGAN

Robust citrus flavors and woodsy rosemary combine to give these olives a lovely, bright flavor. These can be made ahead—up to several days in advance—and the flavors will continue to develop. Serve these with toothpicks—the prettier, the better—for easy enjoyment. Got leftovers? Use them on salads, in martinis, and in wraps.

2 cups pitted green olives, or Kalamata olives

Zest of 1 lemon

Zest of 1 orange

1 tablespoon roughly chopped fresh rosemary leaves

1 garlic clove, minced

¾ cup extra-virgin olive oil

1. In a lidded jar, combine the olives, lemon zest, orange zest, rosemary, and garlic. Drizzle with the olive oil.

2. Put the lid on the jar tightly and shake well to combine. This will encourage the flavors to come together.

3. Let the olives marinate for 30 minutes before serving. If you plan to serve them immediately, leave them at room temperature. If you are making these ahead, chill them until about 30 minutes before you're ready to serve.

PREPARATION TIP: If you plan to serve these immediately, they can also be made in a bowl. Follow the directions, but instead of shaking, stir together to combine.

SWEET AND SPICY ROASTED NUTS

SERVES 8   **PREP TIME:** 5 MINUTES   **COOK TIME:** 20 MINUTES

5 INGREDIENTS | 30 MINUTES | GLUTEN-FREE | MAKE AHEAD | VEGETARIAN

Both sweet and spicy, these nuts are great for snacking. This is a dish to serve with cold beer, such as during a Super Bowl party or March Madness. But don't limit yourself—it's good anytime. Purchase mixed nuts to use here or create your own mix with your favorite nuts.

2 cups raw unsalted mixed nuts

2 tablespoons unsalted butter, melted

2 tablespoons light brown sugar

½ teaspoon kosher salt

½ teaspoon chile powder (see tip)

½ teaspoon crushed dried rosemary

1. Preheat the oven to 350°F. Line a baking sheet with parchment paper and set aside.

2. In a medium bowl, stir together the nuts, melted butter, brown sugar, salt, chile powder, and rosemary until thoroughly combined.

3. Spread the nut mixture on the prepared baking sheet in a single layer.

4. Bake for 15 to 20 minutes, or until the seasoning mixture is liquid and bubbly. Remove from the oven and let cool completely.

5. Transfer the nuts to a serving bowl, breaking up any hard pieces for easier snacking.

INGREDIENT TIP: This recipe calls for chile powder, which is dried ground chiles and comes in varieties such as ancho chile powder and cayenne. *Chili* powder is a different seasoning. It could be used in a pinch but isn't recommended, as its flavor isn't the same.

GOURMET PARMESAN-HERB POPCORN

SERVES 8 **PREP TIME:** 5 MINUTES **COOK TIME:** 5 MINUTES

5 INGREDIENTS | 30 MINUTES | FAMILY FRIENDLY | GLUTEN-FREE | MAKE AHEAD | NUT-FREE | ONE POT | VEGETARIAN

Popcorn is the thing we reach for at the movies and pop for munching while we do homework. Can it also be an upscale party food? Sure it can! With good flavor combinations—sweet, savory, or somewhere in between—popcorn can be elevated from the familiar buttery flavor to something magnificent. This can be made a few hours in advance.

2 tablespoons canola oil

½ cup popcorn kernels

3 tablespoons freshly grated Parmesan cheese

1 teaspoon dried herbs, such as rosemary, thyme, basil, or a combination

Salt

1. In a large pot over medium heat, heat the canola oil.

2. Add the popcorn kernels and cover the pot.

3. Listen for the popping. Let it pop, without moving the pot, until it slows to one pop every 3 to 4 seconds. Then remove the pot from heat and pour the popcorn into a bowl.

4. Sprinkle with the Parmesan cheese and herbs, and season with salt. Stir well to combine, making sure to coat the popcorn evenly with seasoning.

VARIATION TIP: Variations are endless based on your favorite flavor combinations and your imagination. A few to get you started:

- **Chocolate-coated:** Melt some chocolate or white chocolate and drizzle it over the popcorn.

- **Chocolate-flavored:** Sprinkle the popcorn with sweetened hot cocoa mix, to taste.

- **Chocolate–Peanut Butter:** Melt some chocolate or white chocolate and drizzle it over the popcorn along with some peanut butter heated to a pourable consistency.

- **Churro:** Melt 3 tablespoons unsalted butter. Stir in ½ teaspoon ground cinnamon. Drizzle the cinnamon butter over the popcorn. Sprinkle with 1 tablespoon sugar and ½ teaspoon salt. Shake or stir well to combine.

- **Classic Butter:** Melt 2 to 4 tablespoons unsalted butter. Drizzle it over the popcorn. Season with salt.

- **Garlic Butter:** Melt 3 tablespoons unsalted butter. Stir in ½ teaspoon garlic powder. Drizzle the garlic butter over the popcorn and season with salt.

- **Salt and Pepper:** Use a good finishing salt such as pink Himalayan salt or smoked salt with freshly ground black pepper. Use as much or as little as you like, and shake or stir well to combine.

COOKING TIP: This can also be made without oil in the microwave using a paper lunch bag. In a paper bag, combine ½ cup popcorn kernels and ½ teaspoon salt. Roll the top of the bag over a few times, pressing to seal. Place in the microwave and cook for 2 or 3 minutes on high power, or until the popping slows. Remove from the microwave, carefully open the bag, and add the desired seasonings. Close the bag again and shake vigorously.

ROSEMARY-THYME PARMESAN CRISPS

SERVES 8   **PREP TIME:** 15 MINUTES   **COOK TIME:** 20 MINUTES

5 INGREDIENTS | GLUTEN-FREE | MAKE AHEAD | NUT-FREE | ONE POT | VEGETARIAN

Crispy and herbal, these Parmesan crisps are a lovely snack. Serve them alone or use them to garnish other dishes, like risotto or salad. If you make them ahead, let them cool and store in an airtight container at room temperature until ready to serve, or for up to 3 days.

2 cups freshly shredded Parmesan cheese (use a fine shredder)

1 teaspoon crushed dried rosemary

1 teaspoon dried thyme

1. Preheat the oven to 400°F. Line a baking sheet with parchment paper.

2. Spoon 1-tablespoon portions of Parmesan cheese onto the baking sheet, lightly pressing them to spread the cheese out into a round shape. Allow 1 inch of space between the rounds.

3. Sprinkle a pinch of rosemary and a pinch of thyme on each round.

4. Bake for 15 to 20 minutes, or until the rounds are golden at the edges and lightly tanned on the inside.

5. Remove from the oven and let cool for 10 minutes.

6. Repeat until all the cheese has been used.

INGREDIENT TIP: Although these can be made with other cheeses, I don't recommend Romano cheese, which tends to be too sharp for this recipe. Asiago cheese or aged Gouda work well. Also, do not use the pre-grated Parmesan. It won't taste the same.

CHEF'S SALAD SKEWERS

SERVES 8   **PREP TIME:** 15 MINUTES

30 MINUTES | GOOD FOR LEFTOVERS | GLUTEN-FREE | MAKE AHEAD | NUT-FREE

At a recent company party, antipasto salad skewers were the first thing everyone went for. There was something about the meats, cheeses, olives, and veggies on those that caught eyes and drew hands. Inspired, I decided to take one of my favorite salads—the chef's salad—and "skewerize" it, too. Not just for lunch anymore—as a party food, it's divine.

4 ounces sliced turkey deli meat (about 4 slices)

4 ounces sliced ham deli meat (about 4 slices)

4 ounces sliced provolone deli cheese (about 4 slices)

6 large hardboiled eggs, halved widthwise

12 grape tomatoes

1 cucumber, cut into 12 slices

½ head iceberg lettuce, cut into 12 cubes

Balsamic glaze, for drizzling

1. On a work surface, layer one slice of turkey, one slice of ham, and one slice of provolone cheese. Roll them into a tight spiral. Continue with the remaining deli meats and cheese. Cut each roll into 3 pieces.

2. Thread the ingredients onto skewers, in any order you like: 1 roll of deli meat and cheese, ½ hardboiled egg, 1 grape tomato, 1 cucumber slice, and 1 lettuce cube. Continue until all the ingredients have been used.

3. Arrange the skewers in a single layer on a serving platter and drizzle with balsamic glaze.

PREPARATION TIP: To make these ahead, prepare the skewers, but store them in an airtight container in the fridge until ready to serve. Drizzle with balsamic glaze just before serving.

BALSAMIC-DRIZZLED FRUIT AND CHEESE BITES

SERVES 8 **PREP TIME:** 15 MINUTES

30 MINUTES | GLUTEN-FREE | MAKE AHEAD | NUT-FREE | VEGETARIAN

Sweet fruit, creamy cheese, and a bold drizzle of balsamic glaze give these simple but elegant appetizers an edge. The variety of fruits and cheeses make this platter a winner. If you make these ahead, wait to drizzle them with balsamic glaze until just before serving.

2 ounces feta cheese, crumbled

16 fresh raspberries (about ½ pint)

8 fresh strawberries (about ½ pint)

2 ounces fresh mozzarella cheese, cut into 8 pieces

1 apple, cut into 8 wedges

2 ounces Brie cheese, cut into 8 pieces

8 cantaloupe cubes (about 1½ cups)

2 ounces Gouda cheese, cut into 8 pieces

2 tablespoons balsamic glaze

1. Gently push the feta cheese crumbles into the hollows of the raspberries. If desired, skewer with toothpicks—but these stay together on their own, so this isn't required.

2. With toothpicks, skewer together 1 strawberry and 1 piece of mozzarella.

3. With toothpicks, skewer together 1 apple wedge and 1 piece of Brie, with the Brie on top.

4. With toothpicks, skewer together 1 cantaloupe cube and 1 Gouda cube.

5. Arrange the fruit and cheese on a platter for serving. Drizzle with the balsamic glaze.

VARIATION TIP: Additional fruit and cheese pairings can be added to this platter, such as watermelon with feta, apples with Cheddar, and pears with blue cheese.

MARINATED MOZZARELLA WITH SUN-DRIED TOMATOES

SERVES 8   **PREP TIME:** 10 MINUTES, PLUS 10 MINUTES TO MARINATE

5 INGREDIENTS | 30 MINUTES | GLUTEN-FREE | GOOD FOR LEFTOVERS | MAKE AHEAD | NUT-FREE | ONE POT | VEGETARIAN

Creamy fresh mozzarella is marinated in an earthy, spicy, sweet mixture in this recipe. It's a party for the senses, inspired by my favorite olive bar marinated mozzarella. These slices are perfect to serve with crostini, crackers, or just toothpicks. Leftovers are perfect on salads or tucked into wraps.

2 (8-ounce) logs fresh mozzarella, cut into ¼-inch-thick slices

¼ cup roughly chopped fresh parsley

¼ cup sun-dried tomatoes, finely chopped (see tip, page 35)

¼ teaspoon red pepper flakes

1 teaspoon kosher salt

⅔ cup extra-virgin olive oil

1. Place the mozzarella slices in a medium bowl.

2. Top with the parsley, sun-dried tomatoes, red pepper flakes, and salt. Drizzle with the olive oil. Stir until the ingredients are thoroughly combined. Let sit 10 minutes before serving.

PREPARATION TIP: To transform this into a make-ahead recipe, layer half of the mozzarella in a quart jar. Top with the parsley, sun-dried tomatoes, red pepper flakes, and salt. Add the remaining mozzarella and drizzle with the olive oil. Cover the jar, shake thoroughly, and chill. Use within 5 days. Be sure to let sit for 20 minutes at room temperature before serving to allow the olive oil to re-liquefy.

INGREDIENT TIP: Although this is designed to be made with sliced fresh mozzarella logs, mozzarella balls or cubed mozzarella can be used interchangeably.

MARINATED FETA WITH ROSEMARY AND ORANGE

SERVES 8 PREP TIME: 10 MINUTES, PLUS 20 MINUTES TO MARINATE

5 INGREDIENTS | 30 MINUTES | GLUTEN-FREE | MAKE AHEAD | NUT-FREE | ONE POT | VEGETARIAN

This is a dish to serve with toothpicks for stabbing. Salty, creamy feta cheese is flavored with the robust flavors of sweet, citrusy orange and earthy rosemary. Make it ahead for easy serving. Just remember to take it out of the fridge about 20 minutes before you serve it so the olive oil turns to liquid again (it solidifies in the fridge).

12 ounces feta cheese (block form), cut into ½-inch cubes

1 tablespoon roughly chopped fresh rosemary leaves

Zest of 1 orange

1 cup extra-virgin olive oil

¼ teaspoon freshly ground black pepper

1. Arrange the feta in a quart-size jar or covered bowl. Top with the rosemary and orange zest. Stir to combine.

2. Pour in the olive oil and season with pepper.

3. Cover the cheese and let sit at room temperature for 20 minutes before serving. Chill if not using immediately.

VARIATION TIP: For a punchier flavor, add ½ teaspoon red pepper flakes to the mixture.

GREEK SALAD–INSPIRED CUCUMBER BITES

SERVES 8   **PREP TIME:** 15 MINUTES

5 INGREDIENTS | 30 MINUTES | GLUTEN-FREE | MAKE AHEAD | NUT-FREE | ONE POT | VEGETARIAN

Drawing from the flavors of my favorite Greek salads, these cucumber bites are a pretty addition to an appetizer spread. It's the contrasting flavors and textures—cool, crisp cucumbers; soft, salty feta; smooth, sweet roasted red peppers; and firm, salty Kalamata olives—that make them really special.

8 ounces feta cheese (block form), cut into 1-inch rectangles

2 cucumbers, peeled and cut into ¼-inch-thick slices

½ cup sliced roasted red peppers

1 cup Kalamata olives, pitted

1. Layer 1 piece of feta cheese onto each cucumber slice.

2. Arrange a roasted red pepper piece on top of the feta and place the olive in the center of the pepper.

3. Use a toothpick to slide through all the layers and secure the bites.

SERVING TIP: These are so easy to arrange on a platter. Choose decorative toothpicks so they look as good as they taste. To make it extra special, arrange them on a layer of lettuce. You can also offer a light lemony vinaigrette for dipping, if desired.

ROASTED VEGETABLE KABOBS

SERVES 8 **PREP TIME:** 15 MINUTES **COOK TIME:** 15 MINUTES

DAIRY-FREE | GLUTEN-FREE | GOOD FOR LEFTOVERS | MAKE AHEAD | NUT-FREE | VEGAN

Forget boring vegetable platters. These crisp-tender vegetable skewers are a perfect partner with dips, such as Fresh Basil Whipped Feta Dip (page 33) or Sun-Dried Tomato–Garlic White Bean Dip (page 35), or alone. And with their pleasant garlicky flavor, they are a step up from ordinary. These are good served hot or cold.

2 tablespoons extra-virgin olive oil

1 garlic clove, minced

Salt

Freshly ground black pepper

16 cauliflower florets (from 1 head)

16 grape tomatoes (about 1 pint)

16 broccoli florets (about 2 cups)

16 (1-inch) pieces of bell pepper, any color (from 1 pepper)

4 thick scallions, cut into 1-inch lengths

1. Preheat the oven to 400°F. Line a baking sheet with aluminum foil.

2. In a small bowl, whisk the olive oil and garlic until combined. Season with salt and pepper.

3. On each of 16 skewers, thread 1 cauliflower floret, 1 grape tomato, 1 broccoli floret, 1 piece of bell pepper, and 1 scallion piece. Arrange on the prepared baking sheet.

4. Liberally brush the kabobs with the garlic oil mixture. Be sure to use it all, and let the garlic settle on and around the kabobs on the baking sheet.

5. Roast for 12 to 15 minutes, or until the vegetables are crisp-tender and tinged with a golden hue.

VARIATION TIP: Want to change up the veggies? Go ahead. These are also good with zucchini, summer squash, asparagus, and red onion.

CHAPTER THREE

DIPS & SPREADS

AS FAR as appetizers go, dips are the ultimate—easy to make, simple to serve, and almost universally enjoyed. The recipes in this chapter are excellent for serving alone or with other appetizers. Lay out a selection of dippers—such as veggies, slices of bread, crackers, or even chicken skewers—to enjoy with these.

<< LEFT: AVOCADO, MANGO, AND PINEAPPLE SALSA (PAGE 32)

CHUNKY GUACAMOLE

SERVES 8 **PREP TIME:** 10 MINUTES

5 INGREDIENTS | 30 MINUTES | DAIRY-FREE | GLUTEN-FREE | NUT-FREE | ONE POT | VEGAN

Perfectly creamy and deliciously chunky, this guacamole is my specialty. We eat it often on Taco Tuesday, but it's also excellent served with chips or quesadillas for dipping. Make it right before serving for maximum freshness.

2 ripe avocados, halved and pitted (see tip)

½ cup diced tomato

¼ cup diced red onion

¼ cup minced fresh cilantro

Juice of 1 lime

Salt

Freshly ground black pepper

1. Using a spoon, scoop the avocado flesh into a medium bowl. Using a fork, mash the avocado until smooth.

2. Add the tomato, red onion, cilantro, and lime juice. Stir until the ingredients are fully combined. Taste and season the guacamole with salt and pepper.

PREPARATION TIP: The best way to open and pit the avocado is with an avocado tool, if you have one. It ensures you don't accidentally cut yourself while removing the pit. If you don't have one, use a knife to cut open the avocado. Then, whack the pit with the knife and wiggle it gently to remove it.

VARIATION TIP: For added dimension, add ½ teaspoon dried oregano to the guacamole. It's a professional tip I picked up along the way, and I love how it enhances the flavor of this dip.

FRESH TOMATO SALSA

SERVES 8   **PREP TIME:** 10 MINUTES

5 INGREDIENTS | 30 MINUTES | DAIRY-FREE | GLUTEN-FREE | GOOD FOR LEFTOVERS | MAKE AHEAD | NUT-FREE | ONE POT | VEGAN

Hot salsa? Check! This zippy recipe is spicy and fresh. Serve it with chips, quesadillas, or Mini Taco Bites (page 72). And, *if* you have leftovers, try this salsa spooned onto omelets or over baked potatoes—yum!

2 large tomatoes, chopped (about 2 cups)

½ cup diced red onion

1 jalapeño pepper, finely chopped

Zest of 1 lime

Juice of 1 lime

2 tablespoons finely chopped fresh cilantro

Salt

Freshly ground black pepper

1. In a medium bowl (preferably one that can double as a serving bowl), stir together the tomatoes, red onion, and jalapeño.

2. Add the lime zest and lime juice, cilantro, and a sprinkle each of salt and pepper. Mix well. Taste and adjust the seasonings, as desired.

3. This salsa can get a little liquid-y upon sitting. If desired, transfer half the salsa to a food processor and process until smooth. Stir this back into the remaining salsa.

VARIATION TIP: For a milder salsa, remove the seeds and the ribs from the jalapeño before mincing it. This recipe can also be fully puréed for a smoother salsa experience.

AVOCADO, MANGO, AND PINEAPPLE SALSA

SERVES 8   **PREP TIME:** 15 MINUTES

5 INGREDIENTS | 30 MINUTES | DAIRY-FREE | GLUTEN-FREE | GOOD FOR LEFTOVERS | MAKE AHEAD | NUT-FREE | ONE POT | VEGAN

In college, I spent several months in Arizona learning about environmental science and researching. While there, we took a research trip to Mexico, where we had some incredible food—ceviche from a shack in the middle of nowhere, tacos on fresh corn tortillas at an open-air restaurant, and more. Salsas that combine sweet fruits with spicy peppers, like this one, remind me of that time. Good for dipping tortilla chips into, serving with tacos, and more, this fruity salsa comes with a spicy bite. It's a wonderful celebration of contrasts: creamy avocado, sweet mango, tangy pineapple, and spicy jalapeño.

1 avocado, halved and pitted (see tip, page 30)

¾ cup diced mango

¾ cup diced pineapple

1 jalapeño pepper, finely chopped

2 tablespoons minced fresh cilantro

Salt

Freshly ground black pepper

1. Using a spoon, scoop the avocado flesh onto a work surface and dice it. Transfer it to a medium bowl.

2. Stir in the mango, pineapple, jalapeño, and cilantro, stirring until fully combined.

3. Taste and season with salt and pepper.

VARIATION TIP: For a mild salsa, remove the seeds and the ribs from the jalapeño before mincing it.

FRESH BASIL WHIPPED FETA DIP

SERVES 8   **PREP TIME:** 10 MINUTES

5 INGREDIENTS | 30 MINUTES | GLUTEN-FREE | MAKE AHEAD | ONE POT | VEGETARIAN

Salty feta becomes milder and creamier in this whipped dip with a flavor similar to pesto. The addition of ricotta mellows the feta. The bright basil gives this a bold flavor. It's quick to make and enjoy.

6 ounces feta cheese, crumbled

½ cup ricotta

3 tablespoons extra-virgin olive oil, plus more for drizzling

2 tablespoons finely chopped fresh basil

Salt

Freshly ground black pepper

2 tablespoons pine nuts

1. In the bowl of a food processor, combine the feta, ricotta, olive oil, and basil. Process until the mixture appears uniformly smooth. Taste and season with salt and pepper, as desired. Whirl again, if you do so.

2. Transfer the dip to a serving bowl and use a spoon to make a well in the top. Drizzle with additional olive oil and sprinkle with pine nuts.

SERVING TIP: There are so many great ways to serve this dip. Try it with crudités. Offer it with crackers or crostini. Use it as a spread on appetizers or fill the cavities of mini sweet peppers with it.

CARAMELIZED SHALLOT AND PINE NUT HUMMUS

SERVES 8   **PREP TIME:** 15 MINUTES   **COOK TIME:** 8 MINUTES

30 MINUTES | DAIRY-FREE | GLUTEN-FREE | GOOD FOR LEFTOVERS | MAKE AHEAD | VEGAN

A good, basic, creamy hummus with sweet caramelized shallots, this dip is delightful with veggies and crackers, bread, and pita. But it's extra special because of the toppings added before serving—a drizzle of olive oil, a sprinkling of pine nuts, and a dash of caramelized shallots.

4 tablespoons extra-virgin olive oil, divided

2 shallots, halved and sliced

1 (15-ounce) can chickpeas, rinsed and drained

2 tablespoons tahini, or 2 tablespoons sesame seeds

Juice of 1 lemon

1 garlic clove, chopped

2 tablespoons pine nuts, divided

Salt

Freshly ground black pepper

1. In a small skillet over medium heat, heat 1 tablespoon of olive oil.

2. Add the shallots and cook for 6 to 8 minutes, stirring occasionally, until golden.

3. In the bowl of a food processor, combine the chickpeas, tahini, lemon juice, garlic, and 1 tablespoon of pine nuts. Drizzle in 2 tablespoons of olive oil. Add all but 1 tablespoon of the cooked shallots. Process until smooth.

4. If the hummus is too thick for your taste, add water to the processor—1 tablespoon at a time—and whirl after each addition to reach your desired consistency. Transfer the hummus to a serving dish.

5. Drizzle with the remaining 1 tablespoon of olive oil. Sprinkle with the remaining 1 tablespoon of pine nuts and reserved 1 tablespoon of cooked shallots. Season with salt and pepper.

SUN-DRIED TOMATO–GARLIC WHITE BEAN DIP

SERVES 8   **PREP TIME:** 10 MINUTES

30 MINUTES | DAIRY-FREE | GLUTEN-FREE | GOOD FOR LEFTOVERS | MAKE AHEAD | NUT-FREE | ONE POT | VEGAN

Creamy, slightly sweet, and decidedly fragrant, this easy dip is perfect for serving with cucumber slices, cherry tomatoes, pepper slices, cauliflower florets, pita bread, crackers, or crostini. Leftovers are excellent used as a sandwich spread. A rosemary sprig makes a nice garnish.

1 (15-ounce) can white beans, rinsed and drained

¼ cup sun-dried tomatoes

1 garlic clove, peeled

1 teaspoon dried rosemary

½ teaspoon salt, plus more as needed

¼ cup freshly squeezed lemon juice

¼ cup extra-virgin olive oil, plus more for drizzling (optional)

1. In the bowl of a food processor, combine the white beans, sun-dried tomatoes, garlic, rosemary, and salt. Pulse a couple of times to chop.

2. Add the lemon juice and olive oil to the bowl. Process on medium speed for 1 or 2 minutes, or until smooth. Taste and season with more salt, as needed. Transfer to a serving bowl and drizzle with olive oil, if desired.

INGREDIENT TIP: Sun-dried tomatoes can be found in two forms—dried and oil-packed. I prefer the dried ones, which have superior flavor. Look for brands made in Italy, which are usually dried in the sun. Those made domestically are often dehydrated instead of sun-dried (though they carry the same moniker).

SPICY BLACK BEAN DIP

SERVES 8   PREP TIME: 15 MINUTES

30 MINUTES | DAIRY-FREE | GOOD FOR LEFTOVERS | GLUTEN-FREE | MAKE AHEAD | NUT-FREE | ONE POT | VEGAN

Chipotle peppers are a special ingredient. They add so much dimension and richness to dishes with only a small amount needed. In this perfect-for-parties dip, the result is a bold, rich flavor that's wonderful with tortilla chips for dipping but can also stand up to veggies like peppers and cauliflower. Or, try it spread inside a buttered tortilla with shredded Cheddar cheese, folded in half for a tasty take on the quesadilla.

1 (15-ounce) can black beans, rinsed and drained

¼ cup diced red onion, plus more for garnishing (optional)

1 garlic clove, chopped

2 chipotle peppers (from a can of chipotles in adobo sauce)

1 tablespoon adobo sauce (from the can)

1. In the bowl of a food processor, combine the black beans, red onion, garlic, chipotle peppers, adobo sauce, and cumin. Pulse briefly to chop.

2. Add the cilantro, olive oil, lemon juice, and a sprinkling each of salt and pepper. Whirl until smooth. Taste and season with more salt and pepper, as needed. Spoon into a bowl.

1 teaspoon
ground cumin

2 tablespoons minced
fresh cilantro,
plus more for
garnishing (optional)

2 tablespoons
extra-virgin olive oil

2 tablespoons freshly
squeezed lemon juice

Salt

Freshly ground
black pepper

Diced tomato, for
garnishing (optional)

3. Serve garnished with cilantro, diced tomato, or diced red onion, as desired.

VARIATION TIP: For a milder dip with rich flavor, reduce the number of chipotle peppers to one.

HOMEMADE ONION DIP

SERVES 8 **PREP TIME:** 15 MINUTES **COOK TIME:** 15 MINUTES

30 MINUTES | MAKE AHEAD | NUT-FREE | VEGETARIAN

Growing up in the '80s, it seemed like a packet of onion soup mix and a container of sour cream were the secret ingredients to a good party. Just add potato chips, right? But, these days, lots of people are forgoing processed foods for fresh ones, and that can extend to onion dip, too. With a few pantry ingredients, you can make a fresh, homemade onion dip that your guests will adore. Just be sure to cook those onions until they are a very rich golden color for maximum flavor.

2 tablespoons
extra-virgin olive oil

2 cups diced
yellow onion (about
2 large onions)

1 teaspoon salt, plus
more for seasoning

1 (16-oz) container
sour cream

2 tablespoons soy sauce

2 teaspoons
onion powder

2 teaspoons
garlic powder

½ teaspoon paprika

Freshly ground
black pepper

Chopped fresh parsley,
for garnish

1. In a large skillet over medium heat, heat the olive oil.

2. Add the onion and salt. Cook for 10 to 15 minutes, stirring frequently, until the onion is golden. Remove the skillet from the heat.

3. In a medium bowl, stir together the sour cream, soy sauce, onion powder, garlic powder, and paprika until well combined.

4. Stir in the caramelized onion, thoroughly combining it with the dip. Taste and season with salt and pepper, as needed.

5. Transfer to a serving bowl and garnish with parsley.

SERVING TIP: Serve this with your favorite chips for dipping—homemade or otherwise. This can also be served with cucumbers, carrot sticks, celery, and other fresh veggies.

SPINACH ARTICHOKE DIP

SERVES 8   **PREP TIME:** 15 MINUTES   **COOK TIME:** 30 MINUTES

FAMILY FRIENDLY | GOOD FOR LEFTOVERS | GLUTEN-FREE | NUT-FREE | VEGETARIAN

My daughter, a spinach artichoke dip connoisseur, declared this version of the ubiquitous dip the very best she's ever had because it was so thick, creamy, cheesy, and dense with artichokes and spinach. She ended up taking leftovers for lunch in her thermos with some crackers and veggies to dip with. High praise there. I hope you feel the same way.

Cooking oil spray

8 ounces cream cheese, at room temperature

¼ cup sour cream

2 garlic cloves, minced

1 cup shredded mozzarella cheese

1 cup shredded Parmesan cheese

1 teaspoon dried basil

1 teaspoon dried thyme

1 teaspoon kosher salt

½ teaspoon freshly ground black pepper

2 cups frozen chopped spinach

1 (14-ounce) can artichoke hearts, drained and chopped

1. Preheat the oven to 400°F. Spray an 8-by-8-inch square baking dish (or equivalent-size baking dish of any shape) with cooking oil. Set aside.

2. In a large bowl, combine the cream cheese, sour cream, garlic, mozzarella cheese, Parmesan cheese, basil, thyme, salt, and pepper. Stir thoroughly to mix. If necessary, press the mixture with a back of a spoon to force it to combine.

3. Stir in the spinach and artichoke hearts, stirring until thoroughly combined. Transfer the mixture to the prepared baking dish, pressing it into a single layer.

4. Bake for 25 to 30 minutes, or until golden and bubbly at the edges.

5. Serve with vegetables, chips, or crostini for dipping, as desired.

QUICK AND EASY RASPBERRY REFRIGERATOR JAM

SERVES 8   **PREP TIME:** 10 MINUTES, PLUS 30 MINUTES TO MACERATE   **COOK TIME:** 15 MINUTES

5 INGREDIENTS | DAIRY-FREE | FAMILY FRIENDLY | GLUTEN-FREE | GOOD FOR LEFTOVERS | MAKE AHEAD | NUT-FREE | ONE POT | VEGAN

When you make jam yourself, you control everything—from which fruits are used to how sweet it is. This easy jam recipe also speeds up the process by using cornstarch to help it gel. Made with love and perfectly seasoned, this sweet-tart raspberry jam pairs perfectly with the Miniature Baking Soda Biscuits (page 46). It's also a winner used in the Raspberry Baked Brie en Croute (page 76).

2 cups frozen raspberries

¼ cup sugar

2 tablespoons cornstarch

¼ teaspoon salt

1. In a saucepan, combine the raspberries, sugar, cornstarch, and salt. Cover the pan and let sit for 30 minutes. Stir.

2. Place the pan over medium heat. Cook for 13 to 15 minutes, stirring constantly, until the jam is thickened. A spoon pulled through the center should leave a wide wake that takes a bit of time to fill in. Transfer the jam to an airtight storage container. Cover and chill until ready to serve.

VARIATION TIP: This recipe can also be made with different berries. Try blueberries or blackberries, in the same amount as called for here, and proceed with the directions as written.

CHAPTER FOUR

FINGER FOODS

PLATTERS OF easy-to-grab-and-eat foods are so enticing to guests. This chapter is all about finger foods—those eaten by hand in one or two bites. Perfect for piling on plates or just grabbing one to enjoy, these are flavorful bites designed for handheld snacking. Dig into these recipes for more informal gatherings, outside or otherwise, and watch your guests dig in and enjoy.

<< LEFT: ROSEMARY-GARLIC WHIPPED RICOTTA CROSTINI WITH PROSCIUTTO (PAGE 44)

ROSEMARY-GARLIC WHIPPED RICOTTA CROSTINI WITH PROSCIUTTO

SERVES 8   **PREP TIME:** 15 MINUTES   **COOK TIME:** 15 MINUTES

5 INGREDIENTS | 30 MINUTES | NUT-FREE

Ricotta is transformed here into a creamy spread flavored with earthy rosemary and fragrant garlic in this crostini recipe. Spread on little slices of bread and served with a bit of good prosciutto, this is a decadent and impressive appetizer.

¾ cup ricotta

1 garlic clove, chopped

1 teaspoon dried rosemary

Salt

Freshly ground black pepper

1 loaf French bread

Olive oil, for brushing (optional)

4 ounces thinly sliced prosciutto, torn into small pieces

1. In the bowl of a food processor, combine the ricotta, garlic, and rosemary, and season with salt and pepper. Process for 3 or 4 minutes, or until smooth.

2. Preheat the oven to 350°F.

3. Place the French bread directly on the rack and heat for 10 minutes.

4. Cut the warmed bread into ¼-inch-thick pieces. If desired, brush with olive oil and return the slices to the oven for about 5 minutes.

5. Arrange the bread pieces on a serving platter. Top each with a dollop of ricotta and drape with a piece of prosciutto.

TOMATO CAPRESE BRUSCHETTA

SERVES 8   **PREP TIME:** 15 MINUTES   **COOK TIME:** 15 MINUTES

5 INGREDIENTS | 30 MINUTES | VEGETARIAN

The flavors of caprese—tomatoes, basil, and mozzarella—are a summertime favorite. When farmers' markets are brimming with tomatoes of all hues and bushels of bright, inviting basil, this is the dish to make. A spread of good pesto (homemade or otherwise) elevates the flavor. Although this is best assembled right before serving, the bruschetta topping can be made up to a few hours in advance.

1 loaf French bread

1 medium tomato, chopped

4 ounces fresh mozzarella, cut into ¼-inch cubes

1 tablespoon minced fresh basil

Salt

Freshly ground black pepper

Olive oil, for brushing (optional)

¼ cup basil pesto

1. Preheat the oven to 350°F.

2. Place the French bread directly on the rack and heat for 10 minutes. Remove and set aside.

3. In a small bowl, stir together the tomato, mozzarella, and basil. Season with salt and pepper, as desired.

4. Cut the French bread into ¼-inch-thick slices. If desired, brush with olive oil and return to the oven for about 5 minutes.

5. Spread a little pesto onto each bread slice. Top with the tomato mixture. Arrange on a platter and serve.

SERVING TIP: For a pretty presentation, tuck some small sprigs of basil at various points around the platter, between the crostini slices. For an even prettier presentation, nestle clumps of basil leaves around a platter with the crostini when serving.

MINIATURE BAKING SODA BISCUITS FOR A CROWD

MAKES 60 TO 64 BISCUITS   **PREP TIME:** 15 MINUTES   **COOK TIME:** 15 MINUTES

5 INGREDIENTS | 30 MINUTES | FAMILY FRIENDLY | MAKE AHEAD | NUT-FREE | VEGETARIAN

Soft, flaky baking powder biscuits are wonderful. And, for a party, these itty-bitty ones are excellent for serving alongside cheeses, with jam—such as Quick and Easy Raspberry Refrigerator Jam (page 40)—or used to accompany dishes like the Raspberry Baked Brie en Croute (page 76).

2 cups all-purpose flour, plus more for the work surface

1 tablespoon plus 1 teaspoon baking powder

1 teaspoon kosher salt

4 tablespoons cold unsalted butter, cut into pieces

¾ cup milk

1. Preheat the oven to 350°F. Line a large baking sheet with parchment paper. Set aside.

2. In a large bowl, sift together the flour, baking powder, and salt.

3. Add the butter. Using two knives or a pastry cutter, cut the butter into the flour until it resembles coarse crumbs. Make a well in the center of the mixture and pour in the milk. Stir to combine, mixing until a dough begins to form.

4. Flour a board or other work surface and turn the dough out on to it. Knead the dough until it comes together, about 30 seconds to 2 minutes, depending on the temperature of the room and the state of your ingredients.

5. Keeping the board well-floured, use a rolling pin to roll the dough to ¼-inch thickness. Use a 1-inch cookie or biscuit cutter to cut out the biscuits. Gather, knead, and reroll the dough scraps, as needed, to cut the maximum amount

of biscuits possible. Arrange the biscuits on the prepared baking sheet, leaving about ½ inch of space between them.

6. Bake for 12 to 15 minutes, or until the tops begin to turn golden.

7. Remove the biscuits and serve immediately, or cool and store in an airtight container. Serve within 1 day.

COOKING TIP: Cutting butter into flour is a process that uses cold butter and a sharp cutting utensil to cut and mix the butter in. You can use a pastry cutter, which has several blades in a curved shape, or two knives, pulled in opposite directions across the butter. Continue until the butter is in small pieces throughout the flour.

VARIATION TIP: For a buttery top to the biscuits, melt 2 teaspoons salted butter. Brush butter over the tops of the cooked biscuits and return to the oven for 2 minutes more.

CRISPY OVEN-ROASTED PARTY WINGS

SERVES 8   **PREP TIME:** 20 MINUTES   **COOK TIME:** 45 MINUTES

5 INGREDIENTS | DAIRY-FREE | FAMILY FRIENDLY | NUT-FREE

Crispy on the outside, warm and perfectly cooked on the inside—these wings are a party favorite. Serve them tossed in the sauce of your choice, such as barbecue sauce, teriyaki glaze, Buffalo sauce, a mixture of half barbecue and half teriyaki, or sweet chili sauce.

¾ cup all-purpose flour

1 teaspoon kosher salt

½ teaspoon freshly ground black pepper

½ cup canola oil, plus more as needed (see tip)

3 pounds uncooked chicken wings, tips removed and pieces separated

Sauce of choice, for dipping

1. Preheat the oven to 425°F. Line a baking sheet with nonstick aluminum foil or use a nonstick baking sheet.

2. In a shallow wide-bottomed bowl, sift together the flour, salt, and pepper.

3. Place the oil in another shallow bowl.

4. Working with one wing at a time, dip it into the flour mixture, taking care to coat it all over, and dip it into the oil, gently turning to coat. Arrange the coated wing on the prepared baking sheet. Repeat until all the wings have been dipped and coated.

5. Bake for 20 minutes.

6. Using tongs, carefully flip the wings and bake for 20 to 22 minutes more, or until golden on each side.

7. Toss the hot wings with your favorite sauce.

COOKING TIP: It's tempting to try cooking oil spray instead of dipping the wings into oil. Don't do it. They won't get crispy that way. Be sure when you are dipping them in the oil that you thoroughly coat the wings, but do it quickly—you just want a thin outer coating.

STUFFED MINI SWEET PEPPERS WITH WHIPPED FETA

SERVES 8   PREP TIME: 15 MINUTES

5 INGREDIENTS | 30 MINUTES | GLUTEN-FREE | MAKE AHEAD | NUT-FREE | ONE POT | VEGETARIAN

Creamy whipped feta and crisp mini sweet peppers are delightful together in this easy make-ahead recipe. Don't remove the sweet pepper stems. Instead, try to slice through them—they make an easy grabbing point for guests.

2 ounces feta cheese, crumbled

3 tablespoons ricotta

1 tablespoon extra-virgin olive oil

¼ teaspoon freshly ground black pepper

16 mini sweet peppers, halved and seeded

2 tablespoons minced fresh parsley

1. In the bowl of a food processor, combine the feta, ricotta, olive oil, and black pepper. Process for about 2 minutes, or until smooth.

2. Arrange the mini sweet peppers on a platter. Spoon a little of the whipped feta into the cavities of each.

3. Sprinkle with parsley.

VARIATION TIP: Change up the garnish, if desired. For instance, these peppers could also be served with a pinch of grated lemon zest and fresh thyme. Or top them with crispy frizzled onions for a texture difference. You could also finely chop some carrot and cucumber and sprinkle them on top. For a pretty presentation, mix up the toppings between the sweet peppers.

DEVILED EGGS, THREE WAYS

SERVES 8 PREP TIME: 15 MINUTES

5 INGREDIENTS | 30 MINUTES | DAIRY-FREE | FAMILY FRIENDLY | GLUTEN-FREE | MAKE AHEAD | NUT-FREE | VEGETARIAN

This flavorful recipe is lovely served alone, as is—it's a classic! But with the variations, you can turn up the flavor on these bite-size delights.

12 large hardboiled eggs, peeled and halved lengthwise

⅓ cup mayonnaise

1 teaspoon grainy mustard, or Dijon mustard

¼ teaspoon kosher salt

¼ teaspoon freshly ground black pepper

Paprika, for dusting

2 tablespoons finely chopped fresh parsley

1. To make classic deviled eggs, scoop the egg yolks into a medium bowl. Using a fork, mash the yolks into a fine consistency.

2. Stir in the mayonnaise, mustard, salt, and pepper until combined. Transfer the yolk mixture to a pastry bag or a resealable plastic bag. If using the plastic bag, snip off a bottom corner. Pipe the filling into the egg white cavities. If desired, use a fancy pastry tip for a prettier presentation.

3. Sprinkle the eggs with paprika and a pinch of parsley.

VARIATION TIP: It's easy to make variations on the classic recipe—here are two to get you started:

- **Prosciutto and Pesto:** Skip the paprika and parsley, and drape each egg with a piece of prosciutto and drizzle with a little pesto.

- **Lemon Caper:** Skip the parsley. Dust the top of the eggs with paprika. Sprinkle with lemon zest and arrange a few capers on top.

BACON-WRAPPED ASPARAGUS

SERVES 8 **PREP TIME:** 10 MINUTES **COOK TIME:** 15 TO 20 MINUTES PER BATCH

5 INGREDIENTS | 30 MINUTES | DAIRY-FREE | GLUTEN-FREE | NUT-FREE | ONE POT

Crisp-tender asparagus. Crispy bacon. A perfect pairing. This recipe is best made just before serving but will still be good if served at room temperature. If you chill these, they will need to be reheated in a pan over medium heat for 5 to 10 minutes, turning, until hot. This recipe specifies thick-cut bacon—although regular-cut bacon will cook faster, it won't cover the asparagus as well.

1 pound thick asparagus, woody ends removed

½ pound thick-cut bacon, halved crosswise

1. Line a plate with paper towels and set aside.

2. Working with one piece of asparagus at a time, wrap it with one (half) bacon piece. Continue until all the asparagus has been wrapped.

3. Heat a large skillet over medium heat.

4. Working in batches, add the asparagus to the skillet in a single layer, taking care not to overcrowd the skillet. Cook for 3 to 5 minutes per side, flipping and cooking until all sides are browned. Transfer the cooked asparagus to the prepared plate. Repeat with the remaining wrapped asparagus.

SERVING TIP: Sure, you could serve these on a platter. But just think how pretty they would be served in a pint glass.

MEDITERRANEAN MARINATED CHICKEN SKEWERS

SERVES 8   **PREP TIME:** 10 MINUTES, PLUS 30 MINUTES TO MARINATE   **COOK TIME:** 15 MINUTES PER BATCH

DAIRY-FREE | GLUTEN-FREE | MAKE AHEAD | NUT-FREE

Do foods served on sticks just taste better? The jury is out on that one—but I can tell you that everyone who has tried these skewers has fallen in love with them. With the tangy flavor of lemon, warm flavors of basil and oregano, and bold garlic, these marinated chicken skewers are easy for guests to grab and enjoy. They can be served hot or cold.

¼ **cup extra-virgin olive oil**

2 tablespoons apple cider vinegar

1 tablespoon freshly squeezed lemon juice

1 teaspoon dried basil

½ **teaspoon dried oregano**

1 garlic clove, chopped

Salt

Freshly ground black pepper

1½ **pounds chicken tenders**

1. In a small bowl, whisk the olive oil, vinegar, lemon juice, basil, oregano, and garlic until combined. Season with salt and pepper.

2. Arrange the chicken in a lidded bowl. Pour the marinade over the chicken and stir to combine. Cover and refrigerate to marinate for at least 30 minutes.

3. Once marinated, it's time to prepare the chicken for cooking. Remove the chicken from the fridge and thread it onto skewers, one chicken tender per skewer.

4. Heat a grill pan or large skillet over medium heat.

5. Working in batches as needed, cook the chicken skewers for 5 or 6 minutes per side, or until cooked through, flipping once.

VARIATION TIP: These are flavorful enough to enjoy alone. But if you want to offer dipping sauces, vinaigrette and ranch would make good options.

BARBECUE CHICKEN-PINEAPPLE BITES

SERVES 8 **PREP TIME:** 15 MINUTES **COOK TIME:** 20 MINUTES

5 INGREDIENTS | DAIRY-FREE | MAKE AHEAD | NUT-FREE

The sweet and savory combination of chicken and pineapple, brushed with barbecue sauce, makes these skewers a crowd favorite. Although canned pineapple is fine, fresh pineapple really makes these shine. To make these skewers more robust, add a little red onion to each before cooking. These can be served hot from the oven or chilled.

1 pound boneless skinless chicken breast, cut into 1-inch pieces

2 cups pineapple chunks

Salt

Freshly ground black pepper

Paprika, for seasoning

¼ cup barbecue sauce

1. Preheat the oven to 400°F. Line a baking sheet (or two, if you can fit both in your oven) with aluminum foil. Set aside.

2. Thread 2 pieces of chicken and 2 pieces of pineapple onto 1 skewer, alternating chicken and pineapple. Place the skewers on the baking sheet(s). They can be close together but shouldn't touch. Repeat with the remaining chicken and pineapple.

3. Season the skewers with salt, pepper, and paprika.

4. Bake for 10 minutes. Flip the skewers and brush them all over with barbecue sauce. Return to the oven and bake for 5 minutes more.

5. Remove from the oven, flip the skewers again, and brush with the remaining barbecue sauce. Return to the oven for 5 minutes.

6. Arrange the skewers on a platter.

CHICKEN CAESAR SALAD CUPS

SERVES 8   **PREP TIME:** 15 MINUTES   **COOK TIME:** 12 MINUTES

5 INGREDIENTS | 30 MINUTES | FAMILY FRIENDLY | NUT-FREE

Everyone's favorite salad is served in bite-size form in these Chicken Caesar Salad Cups. These are best made just before serving so that the lettuce doesn't wilt too much before guests can try them. However, the chicken can be made ahead.

1 tablespoon
extra-virgin olive oil

8 ounces
chicken tenders

Salt

Freshly ground
black pepper

2 cups finely chopped
romaine lettuce

½ cup shredded
Parmesan cheese

¼ cup Caesar dressing

1 (10-ounce) bag
cup-style tortilla chips

1. In a medium skillet over medium heat, heat the olive oil.

2. Season the chicken tenders all over with salt and pepper. Place them in the skillet and cook for 10 to 12 minutes, flipping once about halfway through the cooking time, until cooked through and golden on each side. Remove the chicken from the skillet and set aside to cool.

3. In a medium bowl, toss together the romaine lettuce, Parmesan cheese, and Caesar dressing until thoroughly combined.

4. Cut the chicken into small bite-size pieces and add them to the bowl. Toss to combine.

5. Arrange the tortilla cups on a serving platter and spoon some salad into each.

VARIATION TIP: Not a fan of tortilla chips? That's okay. This can also be served in shot glasses with little forks. If you do so, consider adding a crouton to the top of each cup for some crunch.

HOW TO ASSEMBLE A CHEESE BOARD

Cheese boards are a fun way to serve a variety of appetizers in a visually appealing way. Use this chart to help you choose your cheese board ingredients and see the tips following it to help you arrange your cheeses. For an excellent cheese plate, choose one or two cheeses from each list along with one meat, two fruits and nuts, and one spread or dip.

SOFT & SEMI-SOFT CHEESES	MEDIUM & HARD CHEESES	MEATS	FRUITS & NUTS	SPREADS & DIPS
Boursin	Asiago	Bresaola	Apple Slices	Apricot Jam
Blue Cheese	Cheddar	Capicola	Apricots, Dried	Balsamic Glaze
Brie	Colby	Dry-Cured Chorizo	Blackberries	Chutney, such as Mango or Red Onion
Cambozola	Edam	Honey Ham	Cranberries, Dried	Grainy Mustard
Camembert	Comté	Hard Genoa Salami	Cherries	Fig Jam
Chèvre (Goat Cheese)	Emmental	Jamón Iberico	Golden Raisins	Honey and Honeycomb
Fontina	Gouda	Jamón Serrano	Grapes	Orange Marmalade
Havarti	Gouda, Aged	Mortadella	Mangoes, Dried	Pesto
Jarlsberg	Grana Padano	Other Cured Sausages	Nuts, such as Almonds, Pecans, Cashews, or Walnuts	Quince Paste
Mozzarella, Fresh	Monterey Jack	Pepperoni	Pear Slices	
Muenster	Manchego	Paté	Olives	Tapenade
Port Salut	Parmesan	Prosciutto	Raspberries	
Taleggio	Pecorino Romano	Soppressata	Strawberries	

A selection of crackers, crostini, bread slices, and breadsticks will complete the cheese board.

To arrange the cheese board, place the cheeses in different sections of the board. Surround with crackers or bread and piles of meats. Add piles of dried fruit or nuts, bowls of dips, spreads, and fruits. Consider the arrangement an art project. Ultimately, you want the board to be full and hearty—and filled with inviting foods.

Serve the cheese board with appetizer plates so guests can take a few items at a time and enjoy them. And feel free to deviate from the list here to create a cheese board spread you love.

CHAPTER FIVE

SAVORY PLATES

A **LITTLE MORE** filling than finger foods and light snacks, savory plates are the appetizers you want to make when you're serving appetizers in lieu of dinner—or planning to have dinner several hours after cocktail hour. These are a little bigger, a little bolder, and totally perfect for providing a more filling element to an appetizer spread. You usually only need to serve one or two of these (along with a few lighter appetizers) to satiate your guests.

<< LEFT: VEGGIE WONTONS (PAGE 68)

PEANUT CHICKEN ENDIVE BITES

SERVES 8   **PREP TIME:** 15 MINUTES   **COOK TIME:** 15 MINUTES

30 MINUTES | DAIRY-FREE | MAKE AHEAD

For the second meeting of our cookbook club, my friend Jillian served what she described as "whatever I had in the fridge" endive bites. The endive leaves held rich bits of hoisin-coated chicken and chopped scallions—delicious. Inspired by her hospitality (and cooking), my version also has a rich sauce. Garlic, ginger, and scallion come together to give this chicken crave-worthy flavor enhanced with the peanuts and more scallions that top it. If you aren't using endive leaves for appetizers yet, now's the time to try it. To make this gluten-free, use tamari in place of soy sauce.

¼ cup chicken stock

1 tablespoon soy sauce

1 tablespoon seasoned rice vinegar

1 tablespoon cornstarch

1 tablespoon extra-virgin olive oil

2 garlic cloves, minced

1. In a small bowl, whisk the chicken stock, soy sauce, vinegar, and cornstarch. Set aside.

2. In a large skillet over medium heat, heat the olive oil.

3. Add the garlic, ginger, and white scallion parts. Cook for 1 minute.

4. Add the chicken to the skillet and cook for 5 to 7 minutes, stirring occasionally, until opaque all over and nearly cooked through.

1 tablespoon grated peeled fresh ginger

5 scallions, thinly sliced, white and green parts separated

1 pound boneless skinless chicken breast, cut into bite-size pieces

1 or 2 endives, leaves separated

2 tablespoons dry-roasted peanuts, chopped

5. Add the sauce to the skillet and cook for 2 or 3 minutes, or until the sauce has thickened and coats the chicken. Remove the skillet from the heat.

6. Spoon the chicken mixture into the endive leaves. Top with a sprinkling of the remaining chopped scallion and the peanuts. These can be enjoyed hot or chilled.

COOKING TIP: These can be made up to 2 days in advance. Store the endive and chicken mixture separately. The chicken mixture should be kept in an airtight container. Wait to chop the scallions until just before serving.

CALIFORNIA TURKEY BURGER SLIDERS

SERVES 8   **PREP TIME:** 15 MINUTES   **COOK TIME:** 15 MINUTES

30 MINUTES | DAIRY-FREE | FAMILY FRIENDLY | NUT-FREE

Creamy, crunchy, salty, and fresh . . . those are all words that describe these divine California Turkey Burger Sliders. Perfect for serving on game night or for evening get-togethers—these little burgers aren't the tiniest bites you'll offer, but they just might be among the most satisfying. These are best made and assembled just before serving.

1 pound ground turkey

Salt

Freshly ground black pepper

1 tablespoon extra-virgin olive oil

8 slider rolls

1 tomato, cut into 8 slices

1 avocado, pitted, peeled, and cut into 8 slices (see tip, page 30)

½ cup fresh spinach leaves, or baby spinach leaves

8 bacon slices, cooked crisp

1. Place the turkey in a large bowl and season it well with salt and pepper. Mix lightly and divide the meat into 8 equal portions.

2. In a large skillet over medium heat, heat the olive oil.

3. While the oil heats, pat each ground turkey portion into a round burger shape about ¼-inch thick. Place the burgers in the skillet. Cook for 8 to 10 minutes, or until cooked through, flipping once about halfway through the cooking time. Transfer to a cutting board or plate.

4. To assemble the burgers, on each slider roll bottom, place 1 burger, 1 tomato slice, 1 avocado slice, one-eighth of the spinach, and 1 bacon slice, torn in half. Top with the upper half of the roll. Serve immediately.

HONEY, HAM, AND BRIE PARTY SANDWICHES

SERVES 6 TO 8   **PREP TIME:** 15 MINUTES   **COOK TIME:** 15 MINUTES

5 INGREDIENTS | 30 MINUTES | MAKE AHEAD | NUT-FREE | ONE POT

The combination of ham and Brie takes me back to eating from street vendors in Paris. And the addition of honey makes these extra special. Baked sandwiches like these are easy to toss together and cook quickly. You can make them just before serving, or assemble them in advance and bake at the last minute. If you make them ahead, wait to brush them with butter until you are ready to bake.

Cooking oil spray

18 Hawaiian rolls, sliced in half lengthwise

8 ounces Brie cheese, rind edge removed (it's okay to leave the rind on top and bottom), thinly sliced

8 ounces deli ham slices

2 tablespoons honey

1 tablespoon unsalted butter, melted

1. Preheat the oven to 375°F. Spray a 9-by-13-inch baking dish with cooking oil.

2. Place the roll bottoms in the prepared dish. Top each with Brie slices and then ham slices, taking care to distribute the ingredients evenly across the rolls. Drizzle with the honey. Top with the roll tops.

3. Brush the melted butter over all.

4. Bake for 12 to 15 minutes, or until the cheese is melty.

5. Let cool for 5 minutes. Using a sharp knife, cut the sandwiches along the roll lines.

VARIATION TIP: Add a seasoned top using sesame seeds, poppy seeds, or everything-but-the-bagel seasoning. After brushing the roll tops with butter, sprinkle with the seasoning before baking.

HUMMUS VEGGIE PINWHEELS

SERVES 8 **PREP TIME:** 15 MINUTES

5 INGREDIENTS | 30 MINUTES | DAIRY-FREE | FAMILY FRIENDLY | MAKE AHEAD | NUT-FREE | ONE POT | VEGAN

In college, a friend and I decided to take charge of our health. In doing so, we started making wraps spread with hummus and filled with veggies. Sometimes we'd also throw in some smoked salmon. They were light but delicious, perhaps even a little comforting. This recipe is inspired by those sandwiches and that time of my life. These are a great two- or three-bite appetizer for parties—especially perfect for warm-weather days.

2 large tortillas, or wraps

½ cup hummus

½ cup grated carrot

½ cup small-dice red bell pepper

½ cup thinly sliced cucumber

1. Lay the tortillas on a cutting board or work surface and spread each with ¼ cup of hummus, spreading it to reach from edge to edge all over in one thin layer.

2. Divide the carrot, red bell pepper, and cucumber evenly between the tortillas, spreading the veggies all over.

3. One at a time, roll up the tortillas, aiming for a tight spiral. Secure the rolls in 5 or 6 places with toothpicks. Cut the rolls into 1-inch pieces, taking care to ensure each is secured with a toothpick (use more toothpicks, if needed).

4. Serve immediately or chill in an airtight container until ready to serve. These can be made up to a day in advance.

VARIATION TIP: Other veggies can be used in these wraps as well, such as green bell pepper, raw summer squash and zucchini, and mesclun mix.

CLASSIC PARTY MEATBALLS

SERVES 8   **PREP TIME:** 15 MINUTES   **COOK TIME:** 25 MINUTES

DAIRY-FREE | FAMILY FRIENDLY | GOOD FOR LEFTOVERS | MAKE AHEAD | NUT-FREE

Sweet and saucy, bold and brilliant, party meatballs have a super-simple two-ingredient sauce and come together with a rich, barbecue-esque flavor. Make these ahead of time and refrigerate for up to 2 days. And don't forget to have toothpicks at the ready for easy noshing!

1 pound ground beef

¼ cup Italian-style bread crumbs

1 teaspoon garlic powder

1 teaspoon onion powder

1 large egg

Salt

Freshly ground black pepper

2 tablespoons extra-virgin olive oil

1½ cups chili sauce

¾ cup apricot preserves

1. In a large bowl, combine the ground beef, bread crumbs, garlic powder, onion powder, and egg. Season with salt and pepper. Stir well to combine. Using clean hands, knead the ingredients together further. Roll the meat mixture into 1-inch meatballs.

2. In a large sauté pan or skillet over medium heat, heat the olive oil.

3. Add the meatballs. Cook for 14 to 16 minutes, turning them a few times, until browned all over.

4. In a small bowl, whisk the chili sauce and apricot preserves. Add the sauce to the skillet and turn the meatballs to coat. Cover the skillet and cook for 10 minutes.

5. Serve immediately, or transfer to a slow cooker set to Warm to keep warm for up to 3 hours.

SHEET PAN PARTY PIZZA

SERVES 8   **PREP TIME:** 15 MINUTES   **COOK TIME:** 20 MINUTES

FAMILY FRIENDLY | GOOD FOR LEFTOVERS | NUT-FREE | ONE POT

This is my favorite thing to make when my kids have friends over because it's so easy and there's something for every pizza lover. By placing different toppings in quadrants, it's like making four different pizzas in one. Plus, by cutting the pizza into strips, it's easy for everyone to enjoy multiple kinds of pizza.

All-purpose flour, for the work surface

1 (usually 1-pound) ball raw pizza dough (often found in the deli section of the grocery store), at room temperature

1 tablespoon extra-virgin olive oil

1 cup marinara sauce

2 cups shredded mozzarella cheese

¼ cup pepperoni slices

¼ cup cooked sausage crumbles

¼ cup diced tomato

1 tablespoon pesto

1. Preheat the oven to 450°F. Line a 9-by-13-inch baking sheet with parchment paper. Set aside.

2. Flour a cutting board or work surface. Place the dough on it and stretch and roll the dough to about the size of the baking sheet. If it shrinks, let it sit for a minute or two and stretch or roll it again. Transfer the dough to the baking sheet and press it to the edges. Prick the dough all over with a fork. Brush the dough with olive oil, including the edges.

3. Spread the marinara sauce all over the dough, leaving about ½-inch border at the edges. Top the dough with the cheese, spreading it all over up to the ½-inch border.

4. On one quarter of the pizza, spread the pepperoni. On a different quarter of the pizza,

spread the sausage. Top another quarter of the pizza with tomato and drizzle the tomato with pesto. Leave the last quarter as just cheese.

5. Bake for 15 to 20 minutes, or until the crust is brown at the edges and the cheese is melted.

6. Remove from the oven and let sit for 5 minutes. Use the parchment paper to help transfer the pizza to a clean cutting board. Cut into strips, about 1-inch wide by 3-inches long.

VARIATION TIP: This can be made with any toppings you like. Try it with ham and pineapple, bacon, broccoli and olives, artichoke hearts, or whatever you and your guests love.

VEGGIE WONTONS

SERVES 8 **PREP TIME:** 45 MINUTES **COOK TIME:** 20 MINUTES

DAIRY-FREE | MAKE AHEAD | NUT-FREE | VEGAN

Crispy fried wonton wrappers conceal a medley of veggies in this make-ahead appetizer. Although these take some time to assemble, they are easy to make, reheat, and serve. Whip up a batch the day before your gathering and toss them in the oven before guests arrive.

FOR THE WONTONS

1 cup grated carrot

1 bunch scallions, thinly sliced, white and green parts (about 1 cup)

1 tablespoon grated peeled fresh ginger

4 garlic cloves, minced

About 30 wonton wrappers (about half of a 12-ounce package)

Canola oil, for frying

FOR THE DIPPING SAUCE

3 tablespoons soy sauce

1½ tablespoons seasoned rice vinegar

To make the wontons

1. In a small bowl, stir together the carrot, scallions, ginger, and garlic, stirring until well combined.

2. Working one at a time, place a wonton wrapper on a cutting board or work surface. Top with about 1 tablespoon of the carrot-scallion mixture. Using a clean fingertip or pastry brush, moisten the edges of the wonton with water and fold the wrapper into a triangle shape. Press the edges together to seal. Repeat with the remaining wrappers and filling.

3. In a large skillet over medium heat, heat about ½ inch of canola oil.

4. Working in batches as needed, carefully add the wontons in a single layer to the hot oil. Cook for 2 or 3 minutes, or until golden. Flip and cook for 2 or 3 minutes more, until the second side is golden. Transfer to a platter and serve with the dipping sauce on the side.

To make the dipping sauce

In a small bowl, stir together the soy sauce and vinegar. Set aside.

COOKING TIP: If you make these ahead, to reheat, spread the cooked wontons on an aluminum foil-lined baking sheet. Bake at 350°F for about 10 minutes. Serve with the dipping sauce.

INGREDIENT TIP: Wonton wrappers can be found in the produce section of most grocers, near the tofu.

CHEESE-STUFFED CHICKEN MEATBALLS MARINARA

SERVES 8   **PREP TIME:** 20 MINUTES   **COOK TIME:** 25 MINUTES

FAMILY FRIENDLY | GOOD FOR LEFTOVERS | MAKE AHEAD | NUT-FREE

Cheese lovers rejoice! These tender, well-seasoned meatballs made of chicken conceal a fun secret: a center filled with gooey mozzarella cheese. Although ground chicken can be tricky to work with—it's juicier than beef or even ground turkey—it's well worth it for these fun meatballs smothered in marinara sauce. Serve these with toothpicks for easy grabbing. If there are leftovers, stuff them in a roll for a delicious sandwich.

1 pound ground chicken

1 cup panko
bread crumbs

1 large egg

½ cup freshly shredded
Parmesan cheese

1 teaspoon dried basil

1 teaspoon dried thyme

1 teaspoon
garlic powder

1 teaspoon
onion powder

1. In a large bowl, stir together the ground chicken, bread crumbs, egg, Parmesan cheese, basil, thyme, garlic powder, and onion powder. Season with salt and pepper. Using clean hands, knead the mixture a bit to mix fully. Form the chicken mixture into 1-inch balls.

2. Working with one ball at a time, flatten it and place 1 mozzarella cube in the center. Reform the meatball around it, sealing completely. Repeat to fill all the meatballs.

3. In a large skillet over medium heat, heat the olive oil.

Salt

**Freshly ground
black pepper**

**2 ounces mozzarella
cheese, (block form)
cut into ¼-inch cubes**

**2 tablespoons
extra-virgin olive oil**

2 cups marinara sauce

4. Add the meatballs. Cook for 14 to 16 minutes, turning occasionally, until browned on all sides.

5. Pour in the marinara sauce, cover the skillet, and cook for 10 minutes.

6. Remove the skillet from the heat. Serve immediately or keep warm in a slow cooker for up to 3 hours.

INGREDIENT TIP: This recipe calls for mozzarella cut from a block, which can usually be found in the dairy case near the bagged pre-shredded cheeses. Do not use fresh mozzarella, which is too soft and watery for this recipe.

MINI TACO BITES

SERVES 8   PREP TIME: 10 MINUTES   COOK TIME: 15 MINUTES

30 MINUTES | FAMILY FRIENDLY | MAKE AHEAD | NUT-FREE | ONE POT

Who doesn't love tacos? In this bite-size version, homemade taco seasoning gives the meat a bold flavor. Top the mini tacos with all the fixings and enjoy this one-bite delight. Or check out the alternative serving idea following to make this a taco bar your guests will adore.

1 pound ground beef

1 tablespoon chili powder

1 teaspoon garlic powder

1 teaspoon ground cumin

1 teaspoon kosher salt

½ teaspoon paprika

⅔ cup water

1 (10-ounce) bag cup-style tortilla chips

1 cup finely shredded Cheddar cheese

1 tomato, chopped

1 cup finely shredded lettuce

1 avocado, peeled, pitted, and diced (see tip, page 30)

Salsa or taco sauce, for serving

1. In a large skillet over medium heat, cook the ground beef for 8 to 10 minutes, breaking it into small pieces, until browned all over.

2. Add the chili powder, garlic powder, cumin, salt, paprika, and water. Stir to combine. Cook for 6 to 8 minutes, stirring, until nearly all the water has evaporated. Remove the skillet from the heat.

3. Spoon a little ground beef into each tortilla cup. Top each with Cheddar cheese, tomato, lettuce, and avocado.

4. Serve with salsa or taco sauce, as desired.

VARIATION TIP: Although these are cute to serve and fun to eat, preparation can take some time. A fun alternative for serving is to set the ingredients up as a taco bar. Instead of tortilla chips, offer the smallest tortillas you can find. The 6-inch soft taco tortillas work great (have 16 to 24 available); if you can find the smaller 4 ½-inch street-taco size, use those. Toppings and the meat should be laid out in separate bowls. If desired, group the bowls on a platter with a stack of tortillas.

BUFFALO CHICKEN WRAPS WITH BLUE CHEESE

SERVES 8 **PREP TIME:** 10 MINUTES, PLUS 10 MINUTES TO COOL **COOK TIME:** 15 MINUTES

5 INGREDIENTS | MAKE AHEAD | NUT-FREE | ONE POT

Fans of Buffalo chicken-anything won't want to miss these wraps. This is one of my favorite appetizers because it combines spicy Buffalo sauce with meaty chicken, creamy but sharp blue cheese, and cool lettuce. As a lover of all things spicy, I find it delightful.

2 teaspoons extra-virgin olive oil

8 ounces chicken breast, diced

Salt

Freshly ground black pepper

¼ to ½ cup Buffalo wing sauce

4 (6-inch) tortillas

½ cup crumbled blue cheese

½ cup shredded lettuce

1. In a small skillet over medium heat, heat the olive oil.

2. Season the chicken all over with salt and pepper and add it to the skillet. Cook for 6 or 7 minutes per side, or until cooked through and no longer pink. Remove the skillet from the heat and let rest for 10 minutes.

3. Add the Buffalo sauce to the chicken and stir to coat.

4. Place the tortillas on a cutting board or work surface. Divide the chicken evenly among the tortillas, spreading it in a line down the center.

5. Top each tortilla with about 2 tablespoons of blue cheese and one-quarter of the lettuce. Roll up the tortillas, securing them with two toothpicks. Cut each in half, cutting straight down.

6. Stand the tortilla halves on their sides to serve, keeping the toothpicks in place.

CHAPTER SIX

FANCY BITES

CONSIDER THIS the elegant chapter. Fancy bites are appetizers with their pinkies out. These are a little more involved, a little more special, and decidedly pleasing to the palate (but aren't they all?) and the eyes. Serve these fancy bites with nicer wines—the fanciness just calls for it. Oh, and skip the paper plates. When you're serving fancy bites, only the finest will do. (Kidding. I'm kidding . . . serve these however you like—but these are well suited for a variety of parties.)

<< LEFT: SHRIMP SATAY WITH PEANUT DIPPING SAUCE (PAGE 82)

RASPBERRY BAKED BRIE EN CROUTE

SERVES 8 **PREP TIME:** 10 MINUTES **COOK TIME:** 25 MINUTES

5 INGREDIENTS | FAMILY FRIENDLY | NUT-FREE | ONE POT | VEGETARIAN

If my kids could choose one appetizer to have every week, this would probably be it. Creamy Brie becomes gooey and melty inside a puff pastry package with sweet raspberry jam in this fun, fancy (but oh-so-easy) dish.

1 sheet frozen puff pastry, thawed

1 (8-ounce) wheel Brie cheese

½ cup Quick and Easy Raspberry Refrigerator Jam (page 40), or store-bought jam

1 large egg, beaten

1. Preheat the oven to 375°F. Line a small baking sheet with parchment paper.

2. Lay the puff pastry in the center of the baking sheet.

3. Place the Brie wheel in the center of the puff pastry.

4. Spoon the jam on top.

5. Fold up the sides of the puff pastry diagonally, pressing to seal. Continue until the Brie and jam are completely concealed.

6. Brush the beaten egg all over the pastry (even beneath the folds!).

7. Bake for 20 to 25 minutes, or until golden brown. Remove and serve immediately with a knife for cutting into and spreading the melty cheese.

SERVING TIP: This is excellent served with Miniature Baking Soda Biscuits for a Crowd (page 46), baguette slices, crackers, or even fruit like apple slices.

CARAMELIZED ONION, MUSHROOM, AND GOUDA PINWHEELS

SERVES 8 **PREP TIME:** 20 MINUTES **COOK TIME:** 40 MINUTES

5 INGREDIENTS | MAKE AHEAD | NUT-FREE | VEGETARIAN

Layers of flaky puff pastry, sweet onion, and meaty mushroom mingle with creamy cheese in this make-ahead appetizer. If you choose to make these ahead, reheat on a parchment paper-lined baking sheet for 10 minutes at 350°F just before serving.

2 tablespoons extra-virgin olive oil

1 medium Vidalia onion, chopped

1 (8-ounce) package sliced fresh mushrooms

Salt

Freshly ground black pepper

1 sheet frozen puff pastry, thawed

1 cup shredded Gouda cheese

1. Preheat the oven to 400°F.

2. In a large skillet over medium heat, heat the olive oil.

3. Add the onion and mushrooms and season with salt and pepper. Cook for 12 to 15 minutes, stirring occasionally. The mushrooms will release their liquid and it will evaporate. The onion will become translucent. When the mushrooms and onion become golden brown, they are ready.

4. Lay out the puff pastry on a cutting board or work surface.

5. Spread the onion-mushroom mixture all over the puff pastry.

6. Top with the Gouda cheese.

7. Roll up the pastry into a tight cylinder. Using a sharp knife, cut the roll into 1-inch pieces and arrange them on a baking sheet.

8. Bake for 20 to 24 minutes, or until golden. Serve immediately.

FIG, GORGONZOLA, AND PEAR TARTLETS

SERVES 8   PREP TIME: 15 MINUTES   COOK TIME: 25 MINUTES

5 INGREDIENTS | MAKE AHEAD | NUT-FREE | VEGETARIAN

Fig jam is a staple of cheese plates, but that's not all it's good for. In these flaky tarts, it complements the pears. The sharp Gorgonzola cheese provides a savory note. These can be made ahead. To reheat before serving, place the tartlets on a parchment paper-lined baking sheet and bake for 10 minutes at 350°F just before serving.

1 sheet frozen puff pastry, thawed

1 ripe pear, cored and diced

¼ cup fig jam

⅓ cup Gorgonzola cheese

1. Preheat the oven to 400°F.

2. Spread the puff pastry on a cutting board or work surface. Using a 3-inch cookie or biscuit cutter, or similar-size object, cut the dough into 12 rounds. Press the dough rounds into the wells of a standard-size muffin tin. You may need to gather and reroll the dough to get a few more rounds.

3. Divide the pear evenly among the dough rounds.

4. Top each with 1 teaspoon of fig jam and a sprinkle of Gorgonzola cheese.

5. Bake for 20 to 25 minutes, or until golden.

6. Use a knife to release the tarts from the sides of the pan. Transfer to a serving plate. Enjoy hot or at room temperature.

SERVING TIP: If desired, sprinkle the tarts with a little extra Gorgonzola cheese before serving. It will increase their savoriness.

POLENTA WITH LEMONY TOMATO BRUSCHETTA

SERVES 8   **PREP TIME:** 10 MINUTES   **COOK TIME:** 20 MINUTES

5 INGREDIENTS | 30 MINUTES | DAIRY-FREE | GLUTEN-FREE | NUT-FREE | VEGAN

Simple ingredients can create elegant outcomes. That's the case with this dish. Crisp polenta is topped with a bright, lemony, herby tomato bruschetta. So simple, and yet so unexpected. Rolls of pre-cooked polenta can be found in most grocery stores near the refrigerated pastas.

2 tablespoons extra-virgin olive oil

1 (18-ounce) roll polenta, cut into ¼-inch slices

1 medium tomato, finely chopped

2 tablespoons minced fresh parsley

Zest of 1 lemon

Salt

Freshly ground black pepper

1. In a large skillet over medium heat, heat the olive oil.

2. Working in batches as needed, add the polenta slices to the skillet in a single layer and cook for 8 to 10 minutes, or until crisp on one side. Flip and cook for 8 to 10 minutes on the other side.

3. Meanwhile, in a small bowl, stir together the tomato, parsley, and lemon zest and season with salt and pepper. Set aside.

4. Arrange the cooked polenta on a serving plate. Evenly divide the lemony tomato bruschetta among the polenta slices.

COOKING TIP: The bruschetta topping can be made up to 2 days in advance and refrigerated in an airtight container.

MINI QUICHE LORRAINE

MAKES 12 QUICHES **PREP TIME:** 10 MINUTES **COOK TIME:** 25 MINUTES

FAMILY FRIENDLY | GOOD FOR LEFTOVERS | MAKE AHEAD | NUT-FREE

There's a good reason people love Quiche Lorraine: It's a classic combination of bacon, eggs, and cheese. But this version is extra special with the addition of scallions and smooth, rich heavy cream. Enjoy any leftovers, reheated, for breakfast or a light lunch.

Cooking oil spray

1 refrigerated piecrust (from a package of 2)

4 thick-cut bacon slices, cooked and crumbled

½ cup chopped scallion, white and green parts

½ cup shredded Cheddar cheese

5 large eggs

½ cup heavy (whipping) cream

Salt

Freshly ground black pepper

1. Preheat the oven to 350°F. Spray 12 wells of a standard-size muffin tin with cooking oil.

2. Spread the piecrust on a cutting board or work surface. Using a 3-inch round cookie or biscuit cutter, or similar-size object, cut out 12 rounds. You may have to gather scraps and re-roll them to get the last few rounds. Press the rounds into the prepared muffin cups, covering the bottom and allowing the dough to extend up the sides (it won't go to the top of the cups).

3. Evenly divide the crumbled bacon among the muffin cups. Top with scallion and Cheddar cheese, dividing them evenly among the cups.

4. In a large bowl, whisk the eggs and the heavy cream thoroughly for 2 minutes. Season well with salt and pepper. Whisk briefly to combine.

Evenly divide the egg mixture among the cups
(the egg mixture will extend above the dough).

5. Bake for 20 to 25 minutes. The egg mixture
should be set and appear a little dry on top.

6. Using a knife, gently loosen the muffin cups.
Remove them from the pan and serve warm.

MAKE-AHEAD TIP: These can be made 2 to
3 days ahead (though they are best when made
the day of serving) and reheated just before
serving. To do so, cook the mini quiches and
remove them from the pan. Refrigerate in an
airtight container. When ready to reheat, preheat the oven to 350°F and put the quiches on
a baking sheet. Heat for 8 to 10 minutes, or until
warmed throughout.

SHRIMP SATAY WITH PEANUT DIPPING SAUCE

SERVES 8   PREP TIME: 15 MINUTES, PLUS 30 MINUTES TO MARINATE   COOK TIME: 10 MINUTES

DAIRY-FREE | GOOD FOR LEFTOVERS | MAKE AHEAD

These shrimp skewers are worthy of a celebration. With a rich marinade, these Thai-inspired shrimp are easy to serve, easy for guests to grab and enjoy, and easy to love. The dipping sauce adds extra depth of flavor. These can be enjoyed hot or cold.

FOR THE SHRIMP

2 garlic cloves, crushed

2 tablespoons soy sauce

1 tablespoon light brown sugar

2 teaspoons Thai fish sauce

1 pound large shrimp, peeled and deveined, tails on

FOR THE DIPPING SAUCE

¼ cup peanut butter

2 tablespoons soy sauce

1 tablespoon sesame oil

1 tablespoon seasoned rice vinegar

1 tablespoon grated peeled fresh ginger

To make the shrimp

1. In a large bowl, stir together the garlic, soy sauce, brown sugar, and fish sauce until well combined.

2. Add the shrimp and stir well to combine. Cover the bowl and refrigerate for at least 30 minutes to marinate, stirring a couple times.

3. Thread 2 shrimp onto each skewer—shorter (6-inch) skewers work best, but any length will work.

4. Heat a grill pan or large skillet over medium heat.

5. Working in batches as needed, place a single layer of skewers in the grill pan. Cook for about 10 minutes, flipping once halfway through the cooking time, until cooked through. The shrimp will be pink and opaque.

6. Serve the skewers on a platter with the dipping sauce in a bowl. Include a spoon so guests can put a little on the skewers—or their plates—as they serve themselves.

To make the dipping sauce

In a small bowl, whisk the peanut butter, soy sauce, sesame oil, vinegar, and ginger until smooth.

COOKING TIP: These skewers can also be roasted. Preheat the oven to 400°F. Arrange the skewers in a single layer on a baking sheet and roast for 5 minutes. Flip and cook for 3 to 5 minutes more, or until cooked through.

CRAB-STUFFED MUSHROOMS

SERVES 8   PREP TIME: 15 MINUTES   **COOK TIME:** 35 MINUTES

MAKE AHEAD | NUT-FREE

A dinner party classic, these fragrant crab-stuffed mushrooms are a crowd favorite. The meaty filling, swirled with veggies and cheese, is a wonderful foil to the earthy mushrooms.

Cooking oil spray

24 ounces cremini mushrooms, cleaned and stemmed, stems reserved

1 tablespoon extra-virgin olive oil

⅓ cup minced red bell pepper

¼ cup minced red onion

2 garlic cloves, minced

½ teaspoon paprika

½ teaspoon dried thyme

1 (6-ounce) can crabmeat, drained

½ cup grated Gouda cheese

3 tablespoons panko bread crumbs, divided

Salt

Freshly ground black pepper

1. Preheat the oven to 350°F. Spray a 9-by-13-inch glass baking dish with cooking oil.

2. Arrange the mushrooms, stem-side up, in the prepared baking dish.

3. Finely chop the reserved mushroom stems to get ⅓ cup. Discard the remainder.

4. In a large skillet over medium heat, heat the olive oil.

5. Add the mushroom stems, red bell pepper, and red onion. Cook for 6 or 7 minutes, or until soft.

6. Add the garlic and cook for 1 minute, or until fragrant. Transfer the vegetable mixture to a medium bowl.

7. Add the paprika, thyme, crabmeat, Gouda cheese, and 1 tablespoon of panko to the cooked vegetables and season with salt and pepper. Stir together until well combined.

8. Evenly divide the crab stuffing among the mushroom caps. Sprinkle the tops with the remaining panko.

9. Bake for 20 to 25 minutes, or until the mushrooms have darkened in color and the tops are beginning to brown. Serve warm.

COOKING TIP: These can be made a few hours ahead of time and reheated in a 350°F oven for 8 to 10 minutes, or until warm.

GARLIC-GINGER PORTOBELLO MUSHROOMS

SERVES 8   PREP TIME: 10 MINUTES   COOK TIME: 10 MINUTES

30 MINUTES | DAIRY-FREE | MAKE AHEAD | NUT-FREE | ONE POT | VEGAN

Portobello mushrooms are so versatile. They have a meatiness that makes them perfect for serving in sandwiches, stuffing, or even swirling into ramen. These mushrooms are sweet, spicy, and richly flavored with garlic and ginger. They are great eaten alone—serve with toothpicks for grabbing—but, if you have leftovers, toss them on rice bowls or tuck them into wraps.

2 tablespoons extra-virgin olive oil

2 garlic cloves, minced

1 tablespoon grated peeled fresh ginger

2 tablespoons seasoned rice vinegar

2 tablespoons soy sauce

1 tablespoon light brown sugar

¼ teaspoon red pepper flakes

2 portobello mushrooms, cut into ¼-inch-thick slices

2 tablespoons finely chopped or snipped fresh chives

1. In a medium skillet over medium heat, heat the olive oil.

2. Add the garlic and ginger and cook for 2 minutes.

3. Whisk in the vinegar, soy sauce, brown sugar, and red pepper flakes. Cook for 1 minute.

4. Add the mushroom slices to the skillet and cook for 6 or 7 minutes, stirring occasionally, until the sauce is thickened and the mushrooms are dark in color. Remove the skillet from the heat.

5. Arrange the mushrooms on a platter and sprinkle with the chives.

SERVING TIP: These would also be good served with pitas, veggies, and other toppings for build-your-own sandwiches.

SUBSTITUTION TIP: A thinly sliced scallion can be used in place of chives.

SALMON FRITTERS

SERVES 8   PREP TIME: 10 MINUTES   COOK TIME: 25 MINUTES

DAIRY-FREE | GLUTEN-FREE | MAKE AHEAD | NUT-FREE

Sometimes, the best recipes are the unexpected ones. This was a happy surprise. While testing salmon cake recipes, I ran out of bread crumbs and, instead, reached for cornmeal. Once everything was combined, I realized I might be onto something—cornmeal worked perfectly as a binder and added a bit of unique flavor and texture. These lemony, fragrant fritters are great served with cocktail sauce for dipping.

2 (5-ounce) cans salmon, drained

½ cup cornmeal

2 large eggs, beaten

2 garlic cloves, minced

Zest of 1 lemon

Juice of 1 lemon

2 scallions, thinly sliced, white and green parts separated

Salt

Freshly ground black pepper

3 tablespoons extra-virgin olive oil

1. In a large bowl, combine the salmon, cornmeal, eggs, garlic, lemon zest, lemon juice, and scallion whites and season with salt and pepper. Stir until the ingredients are well combined.

2. In a large skillet over medium heat, heat the olive oil.

3. Working in batches, drop the salmon mixture into the skillet by the tablespoonful. Cook until the edges of the fritters begin to brown, about 6 minutes. Flip and cook until the second side is browned, about 6 minutes more. Transfer to a serving plate and sprinkle with the remaining scallions. Serve hot.

COOKING TIP: The salmon mixture can be made ahead of time and chilled until ready to cook.

CRISPY GARLIC BUTTER SMASHED POTATOES

SERVES 8   **PREP TIME:** 10 MINUTES   **COOK TIME:** 55 MINUTES

5 INGREDIENTS | FAMILY FRIENDLY | GLUTEN-FREE | MAKE AHEAD | NUT-FREE | VEGETARIAN

Buttery, garlicky potatoes with crisp edges and soft insides, these itty-bitty potato treats will entice. These can be finger foods, but they're almost better served with forks so you can savor them in smaller bites.

3 pounds yellow new potatoes, or fingerling potatoes

1 tablespoon extra-virgin olive oil

3 tablespoons unsalted butter, melted

2 garlic cloves, minced

Salt

Freshly ground black pepper

2 tablespoons finely chopped fresh parsley

1. Boil the potatoes in a large pot of water over high heat for 20 to 25 minutes, or until tender. Drain.

2. Preheat the oven to 425°F. Line a baking sheet with parchment paper and brush the parchment with olive oil.

3. Place the potatoes on the baking sheet and smash with a fork or a potato masher. Drizzle with the melted butter and sprinkle with the garlic. Season with salt and pepper.

4. Bake for 25 to 30 minutes, or until the potatoes are golden and crisp at the edges and in places across the top. They will be firm on the outside and soft on the inside.

5. Remove the potatoes from the oven and let cool for 5 minutes. Transfer to a serving tray and sprinkle with parsley.

COOKING TIP: If you make these ahead, reheat at 350°F for about 10 minutes.

CHAPTER SEVEN

SOMETHING SWEET

END YOUR gathering on a sweet note with a bite-size appetizer like the ones in this chapter. With everything from lighter bites to more indulgent ones, these recipes are designed to tantalize your taste buds and tingle your senses. Make one dessert or several—whatever you like. And consider serving these with a side of coffee or tea.

<< LEFT: MINI APPLE PIES WITH CRUMB TOPPING (PAGE 102)

RASPBERRY-WATERMELON SMOOTHIE SHOOTERS

SERVES 8   **PREP TIME:** 15 MINUTES

5 INGREDIENTS | 30 MINUTES | FAMILY FRIENDLY | GLUTEN-FREE | NUT-FREE | ONE POT | VEGETARIAN

Dessert doesn't have to be heavy or filled with butter, and these adorable smoothie shooters are proof—fruity, creamy, and refreshing proof. Plus, they're too pretty to pass up.

2 cups ice

2 cups watermelon cubes, plus more for garnishing

1 pint fresh raspberries, plus more for garnishing

¾ cup milk

1. In a blender, combine the ice, watermelon cubes, raspberries, and milk (in that order). Blend for about 2 minutes on high speed, or until smooth.

2. Pour the smoothie into small (shot or slightly larger) glasses.

3. Garnish, as desired, with a raspberry or watermelon cube. To do so, cut a slit in the fruit and slide it onto the rim of the glass.

PREPARATION TIP: These smoothies are best made just before serving so they are perfectly blended and chilled.

FRUIT SKEWERS WITH CREAMY MARSHMALLOW DIP

SERVES 8   **PREP TIME:** 20 MINUTES

30 MINUTES | FAMILY FRIENDLY | GLUTEN-FREE | GOOD FOR LEFTOVERS | MAKE AHEAD | NUT-FREE | VEGETARIAN

A delicious dessert does not have to be complicated. This easy, tasty dessert features fresh fruit primed for dipping in a creamy marshmallow dip. This dip was super popular in the early 2000s at parties—and is as tasty today. The dip can be made up to 2 days in advance and refrigerated. Let it sit at room temperature for 30 minutes before serving. The skewers should be made the day of your gathering and chilled until ready to serve.

FOR THE FRUIT SKEWERS

1 quart strawberries, hulled

2 cups cubed melon (watermelon, cantaloupe, or honeydew)

1 cup seedless red grapes

1 cup seedless green grapes

1 cup pineapple cubes

FOR THE MARSHMALLOW DIP

8 ounces cream cheese, at room temperature

7 ounces marshmallow creme

1 tablespoon grated orange zest

To make the fruit skewers

Arrange 3 or 4 pieces of fruit on a skewer. Repeat with more skewers and the remaining fruit until all the fruit has been used (you'll have about 15 skewers). For best results, vary the fruit combinations so folks have options. Arrange the fruit skewers on a large platter with a bowl for the dip in the center.

To make the marshmallow dip

In a medium bowl, whisk the cream cheese, marshmallow creme, and orange zest until smooth. Spoon into the serving bowl and place it in the center of the platter.

INGREDIENT TIP: To make this recipe vegetarian, buy vegetarian marshmallow creme.

DOUBLE-CHOCOLATE BROWNIE BITES

SERVES 8   **PREP TIME:** 15 MINUTES   **COOK TIME:** 15 MINUTES

30 MINUTES | FAMILY FRIENDLY | GOOD FOR LEFTOVERS | MAKE AHEAD | NUT-FREE | VEGETARIAN

Rich and chocolatey, these brownie bites are a crowd-pleaser. Bake them 15 minutes for cakier brownies, or 12 minutes for fudgier ones. Leftovers can be stored in an airtight container for up to 5 days.

2 ounces dark chocolate, chopped

4 tablespoons unsalted butter

½ cup sugar

2 large eggs, beaten

1 teaspoon vanilla extract

½ cup all-purpose flour

½ teaspoon baking powder

½ teaspoon kosher salt

½ cup semisweet chocolate chips

1. Preheat the oven to 375°F. Line 24 mini cupcake cups with liners and set aside.

2. In a small saucepan over medium heat, combine the dark chocolate and butter. Warm, stirring constantly, until smooth, 4 to 6 minutes. Remove the pan from the heat.

3. In a large bowl, whisk the sugar, eggs, and vanilla.

4. While still hot, drizzle the chocolate into the sugar mixture in a thin stream, whisking constantly, until fully combined. Adding the hot chocolate mixture in a thin stream will temper the eggs, allowing it to incorporate without cooking them.

5. In a small bowl, sift together the flour, baking powder, and salt. Add the dry ingredients to the chocolate mixture and stir to combine.

6. Stir in the chocolate chips. Divide the batter evenly among the prepared cupcake liners.

7. Bake for 12 to 15 minutes. When done, the tops will look dry. Cool slightly before serving.

SUBSTITUTION TIP: Instead of dark chocolate, use an equal amount of unsweetened baking chocolate or milk chocolate.

SALTED PEANUT BUTTER COOKIES

MAKES ABOUT 30 COOKIES   **PREP TIME:** 15 MINUTES   **COOK TIME:** 10 MINUTES PER BATCH

30 MINUTES | FAMILY FRIENDLY | GOOD FOR LEFTOVERS | MAKE AHEAD | VEGETARIAN

Fork & Spoon, a bakery in Bangor, Maine, sells giant salted chocolate chip cookies that are just divine. These are a riff on that favorite dessert, a bit smaller but decidedly satisfying. The salt on these familiar cookies makes them stand out from the cookie crowd.

1 cup peanut butter

8 tablespoons (1 stick) unsalted butter, at room temperature

½ cup packed light brown sugar

½ cup granulated sugar

1 large egg

1 cup all-purpose flour

1 teaspoon baking soda

¼ teaspoon salt, plus more for sprinkling

1. Preheat the oven to 375°F. Line a baking sheet with parchment paper and set aside.

2. In the bowl of a stand mixer, or in a large bowl and using a handheld electric mixer, beat together the peanut butter, butter, brown sugar, and granulated sugar until fully incorporated. The mixture should be light and almost fluffy.

3. Add the egg and mix well to combine.

4. In a medium bowl, sift together the flour, baking soda, and salt.

5. With the mixer running on its lowest speed, little by little, add the flour to the peanut butter mixture and mix until fully incorporated. You may need to stop to scrape down the sides of the bowl midway through mixing.

6. Drop the cookie dough by the tablespoonful onto the prepared baking sheet, allowing 2 inches between lumps. A medium cookie scoop is perfect for this. Use the prongs of a fork to press the dough with the familiar crisscross pattern. Sprinkle each cookie with a pinch of salt.

7. Bake for 8 to 10 minutes, or until golden at the edges.

8. Let the cookies cool on the baking sheet for 5 minutes before transferring to a wire rack to cool completely.

9. Repeat until all the dough has been used.

PREPARATION TIP: These cookies are pretty soft, so be sure to store them carefully.

CINNAMON SWIRL MINI CUPCAKES

SERVES 8 **PREP TIME:** 30 MINUTES **COOK TIME:** 20 MINUTES

FAMILY FRIENDLY | GOOD FOR LEFTOVERS | MAKE AHEAD | NUT-FREE | VEGETARIAN

A ribbon of cinnamon filling—not unlike your favorite cinnamon roll—makes these mini cupcakes divine. And the creamy vanilla frosting complements the flavor so well. Although these cupcakes take longer to make than some other recipes in this book, they can be made up to a day in advance.

FOR THE CUPCAKES

1 cup all-purpose flour

½ cup plus 2 tablespoons granulated sugar

1 teaspoon baking powder

¾ teaspoon baking soda

½ teaspoon kosher salt

1 large egg

½ cup milk

¼ cup canola oil

½ teaspoon ground cinnamon

To make the cupcakes

1. Preheat the oven to 375°F. Line 24 mini muffin cups with liners and set aside.

2. In a medium bowl, sift together the flour, ½ cup of granulated sugar, baking powder, baking soda, and salt.

3. Whisk the egg, milk, and oil into the flour mixture, continuing to whisk vigorously for 2 minutes, or until smooth. Add enough batter to the prepared liners to cover the bottom of each. (You should use about half the batter.)

4. In a small bowl, stir together the remaining 2 tablespoons of granulated sugar and cinnamon. Evenly divide this filling among the cupcakes.

5. Evenly top each with the remaining batter.

6. Bake for 15 to 18 minutes, or until a cake tester inserted into the center of a cupcake comes out clean.

7. Transfer the cupcakes to a wire rack and cool fully.

FOR THE VANILLA FROSTING

8 tablespoons (1 stick) unsalted butter, cold

1½ cups confectioners' sugar

2 tablespoons marshmallow creme

1 teaspoon vanilla extract

To make the vanilla frosting

1. In the bowl of a stand mixer with the wire whip attached, or in a large bowl and using a handheld electric mixer, beat the cold butter for about 2 minutes on medium speed, until light and fluffy.

2. Add the confectioners' sugar, marshmallow creme, and vanilla. Beat on low speed to incorporate. Once fluffy and fully combined, transfer the frosting to a pastry bag—or a resealable plastic bag, snipping off one bottom corner—and pipe the frosting onto the cooled cupcakes.

CHOCOLATE CHIP MINI CHEESECAKES

MAKES 20 CHEESECAKES   **PREP TIME:** 15 MINUTES   **COOK TIME:** 20 MINUTES

FAMILY FRIENDLY | GOOD FOR LEFTOVERS | MAKE AHEAD | NUT-FREE | VEGETARIAN

Growing up in New York, one of my favorite treats was cheesecake—especially creative versions that turned the traditional plain cheesecake into something more exciting. These itty-bitty cheesecakes are a bite-size version of that favorite dessert. Dotted with chocolate chips, your guests will love them.

2 (8-ounce) packages cream cheese, at room temperature

3 large eggs

1 cup sugar

1 teaspoon vanilla extract

¼ teaspoon kosher salt

1 cup semisweet chocolate chips

20 vanilla wafers

1. Preheat the oven to 350°F. Line 20 wells of standard-size muffin tins with cupcake liners.

2. In the bowl of a stand mixer fitted with the paddle attachment, or in a large bowl and using a handheld electric mixer, combine the cream cheese, eggs, sugar, vanilla, and salt. Starting on the lowest speed and working your way up to high speed, little by little, mix until smooth (you'll have minimal mess this way).

3. Add the chocolate chips and mix briefly to combine.

4. Place 1 vanilla wafer in each of the cupcake liners. Fill each about two-thirds full of cheesecake batter (or divide it evenly among the 20 liners).

5. Bake for 15 to 20 minutes, or until golden at the edges.

6. Remove from the oven and cool the cheesecakes for 20 minutes before removing them from the pan.

7. Chill until ready to serve. These can be made up to 3 days in advance.

VARIATION TIP: These are great served as is, but for a special treat, top with strawberries in syrup.

MINI APPLE PIES WITH CRUMB TOPPING

MAKES 12 PIES   **PREP TIME:** 15 MINUTES   **COOK TIME:** 20 MINUTES

FAMILY FRIENDLY | MAKE AHEAD | NUT-FREE | VEGETARIAN

Bite-size desserts are a fun way to enjoy favorites. In this case, apple pie gets a mini makeover with a sweet, buttery crumb topping. This is especially great for fall tailgating.

1 refrigerated piecrust (from a package of 2)

2 apples, cored and diced

2 tablespoons granulated sugar

¼ cup plus 1 tablespoon all-purpose flour, divided

1 teaspoon ground cinnamon

¼ cup packed light brown sugar

2 tablespoons unsalted butter, melted

1. Preheat the oven to 425°F.

2. Place the piecrust on a cutting board or work surface. Using a 4-inch round cookie or biscuit cutter, or other similar-size object, cut the dough into 12 rounds and press them into the wells of a standard-size muffin tin. Continue until all the dough has been used. You may need to gather and re-roll the scraps for the last few rounds.

3. In a medium bowl, stir together the apples, granulated sugar, 1 tablespoon of flour, and the cinnamon until fully combined. Spoon the apple filling into the dough rounds, evenly dividing it among them.

4. In a small bowl, stir together the remaining ¼ cup of flour and brown sugar. Drizzle in the melted butter and mix well to combine. Spoon the topping over the pies, dividing it evenly among them.

5. Bake for 18 to 20 minutes, or until golden on top.

6. Let the pies cool for 30 minutes in the pan before loosening them with a knife and transferring to a wire rack to cool completely.

SERVING TIP: A dollop of vanilla ice cream on top or a bit of whipped cream is delicious.

GLAZED STRAWBERRY TARTLETS

SERVES 8   **PREP TIME:** 10 MINUTES   **COOK TIME:** 5 MINUTES

5 INGREDIENTS | 30 MINUTES | DAIRY-FREE | FAMILY FRIENDLY | NUT-FREE | VEGAN

Fresh strawberries are such a treat—and so are these sweet, fresh tartlets. Quick, simple, and fun, these are best made at the last minute.

¼ cup apricot preserves

1 teaspoon water

1 cup diced
fresh strawberries

1 package phyllo shells
(15 shells)

1. In a small saucepan over medium heat, stir together the apricot preserves and water. Heat until it reaches a pourable consistency, about 5 minutes.

2. Place the strawberries in a medium bowl and drizzle the apricot mixture over them. Toss well to combine.

3. Arrange the phyllo shells on a serving plate.

4. Evenly divide the strawberry mixture among them. Serve immediately.

PREPARATION TIP: The phyllo shells do not need to be thawed before using.

S'MORES TARTS

SERVES 8   **PREP TIME:** 5 MINUTES   **COOK TIME:** 3 MINUTES

5 INGREDIENTS | 30 MINUTES | FAMILY FRIENDLY | NUT-FREE | ONE POT

A nod to campfire classics, these are the grownup version of that childhood favorite. Although these can't be made ahead, per se, they can be prepared ahead for baking. Arrange all the ingredients in the shells on a parchment paper-lined baking sheet. Slide into the oven just before serving.

8 dessert shells (see tip)

3 ounces chocolate, chopped

2 graham crackers, each broken into 4 smaller rectangles along the perforations

8 marshmallows

1. Preheat the broiler to high with the top rack set 6 inches from it. Line a baking sheet with parchment paper.

2. Lay out the dessert shells on the prepared baking sheet. Fill each with an equal amount of chocolate.

3. Crumble 1 graham cracker rectangle onto each and top each with 1 marshmallow, nestling it on top.

4. Carefully slide the baking sheet into the oven and close the door. Stay close by, though—check these after 30 seconds and again at 1 minute. When the marshmallow is browned, these should be removed from the oven. Serve immediately.

INGREDIENT TIP: Look for dessert shells in the bakery section, or in the produce section, often near the fresh berries.

CINNAMON SUGAR PINWHEELS

SERVES 8   **PREP TIME:** 15 MINUTES   **COOK TIME:** 20 MINUTES

5 INGREDIENTS | FAMILY FRIENDLY | GOOD FOR LEFTOVERS | MAKE AHEAD | NUT-FREE | VEGETARIAN

Bursting with cinnamon-sugar flavor, these flaky cookies feel elegant but are ridiculously easy to make. Whip up a batch the day before your event and store them at room temperature until ready to serve.

1 sheet frozen puff pastry, thawed

1 tablespoon unsalted butter, melted

¼ cup sugar

1 teaspoon ground cinnamon

1. Preheat the oven to 400°F. Line a baking sheet with parchment paper. Set aside.

2. Lay the puff pastry on a cutting board or work surface and brush it with the melted butter.

3. In a small bowl, stir together the sugar and cinnamon. Sprinkle the cinnamon-sugar all over the buttered puff pastry. Tightly roll up the puff pastry into a cylinder.

4. Using a sharp knife, cut the roll into ¼-inch-thick slices. Arrange them on the prepared baking sheet, allowing about 1 inch between rounds. Sprinkle with any cinnamon-sugar that fell out of the roll during cutting or transfer.

5. Bake for 15 to 20 minutes, or until golden.

6. Remove from the oven. Let cool for 5 minutes and transfer the cookies to a wire rack to cool fully. Store at room temperature in an airtight container.

THE DIRTY DOZEN™ AND THE CLEAN FIFTEEN™

A NONPROFIT environmental watchdog organization called Environmental Working Group (EWG) looks at data supplied by the US Department of Agriculture (USDA) and the Food and Drug Administration (FDA) about pesticide residues. Each year it compiles a list of the best and worst pesticide loads found in commercial crops. You can use these lists to decide which fruits and vegetables to buy organic to minimize your exposure to pesticides and which produce is considered safe enough to buy conventionally. This does not mean they are pesticide-free, though, so wash these fruits and vegetables thoroughly. The list is updated annually, and you can find it online at EWG.org/FoodNews.

DIRTY DOZEN™

1. strawberries
2. spinach
3. kale
4. nectarines
5. apples
6. grapes
7. peaches
8. cherries
9. pears
10. tomatoes
11. celery
12. potatoes

Additionally, nearly three-quarters of hot pepper samples contained pesticide residues.

CLEAN FIFTEEN™

1. avocados
2. sweet corn
3. pineapples
4. sweet peas (frozen)
5. onions
6. papayas
7. eggplants
8. asparagus
9. kiwis
10. cabbages
11. cauliflower
12. cantaloupes
13. broccoli
14. mushrooms
15. honeydew melons

MEASUREMENT CONVERSIONS

Volume Equivalents (Liquid)

Standard	US Standard (ounces)	Metric (approximate)
2 tablespoons	1 fl. oz.	30 mL
¼ cup	2 fl. oz.	60 mL
½ cup	4 fl. oz.	120 mL
1 cup	8 fl. oz.	240 mL
1½ cups	12 fl. oz.	355 mL
2 cups or 1 pint	16 fl. oz.	475 mL
4 cups or 1 quart	32 fl. oz.	1 L
1 gallon	128 fl. oz.	4 L

Oven Temperatures

Fahrenheit (F)	Celsius (C) (approximate)
250°	120°
300°	150°
325°	165°
350°	180°
375°	190°
400°	200°
425°	220°
450°	230°

Volume Equivalents (Dry)

Standard	Metric (approximate)
⅛ teaspoon	0.5 mL
¼ teaspoon	1 mL
½ teaspoon	2 mL
¾ teaspoon	4 mL
1 teaspoon	5 mL
1 tablespoon	15 mL
¼ cup	59 mL
⅓ cup	79 mL
½ cup	118 mL
⅔ cup	156 mL
¾ cup	177 mL
1 cup	235 mL
2 cups or 1 pint	475 mL
3 cups	700 mL
4 cups or 1 quart	1 L

Weight Equivalents

Standard	Metric (approximate)
½ ounce	15 g
1 ounce	30 g
2 ounces	60 g
4 ounces	115 g
8 ounces	225 g
12 ounces	340 g
16 ounces or 1 pound	455 g

INDEX

A

Afternoon parties, 4–5, 10

Apples
Balsamic-Drizzled Fruit and Cheese Bites, 23
Mini Apple Pies with Crumb Topping, 102–103

Artichoke Spinach Dip, 39

Asparagus, Bacon-Wrapped, 52

Avocados
Avocado, Mango, and Pineapple Salsa, 32
California Turkey Burger Sliders, 62
Chunky Guacamole, 30
Mini Taco Bites, 72

B

Bacon
Bacon-Wrapped Asparagus, 52
California Turkey Burger Sliders, 62
Mini Quiche Lorraine, 80–81

Balsamic-Drizzled Fruit and Cheese Bites, 23

Barbecue Chicken-Pineapple Bites, 54

Basil
Fresh Basil Whipped Feta Dip, 33
Tomato Caprese Bruschetta, 45

Beans
Spicy Black Bean Dip, 36–37
Sun-Dried Tomato-Garlic White Bean Dip, 35

Beef
Classic Party Meatballs, 65
Mini Taco Bites, 72

Berries
Balsamic-Drizzled Fruit and Cheese Bites, 23
Fruit Skewers with Creamy Marshmallow Dip, 93
Glazed Strawberry Tartlets, 104
Quick and Easy Raspberry Refrigerator Jam, 40
Raspberry Baked Brie en Croute, 76
Raspberry-Watermelon Smoothie Shooters, 92

Beverages, 10–11

Biscuits, Miniature Baking Soda, for a Crowd, 46–47

Blue Cheese, Buffalo Chicken Wraps with, 73

Bread. See also Rolls
Rosemary-Garlic Whipped Ricotta Crostini with Prosciutto, 44
Tomato Caprese Bruschetta, 45

Brie cheese
Balsamic-Drizzled Fruit and Cheese Bites, 23
Honey, Ham, and Brie Party Sandwiches, 63
Raspberry Baked Brie en Croute, 76

Broccoli
Roasted Vegetable Kabobs, 27

Brownie Bites, Double-Chocolate, 94–95

Bruschetta
Polenta with Lemony Tomato Bruschetta, 79
Tomato Caprese Bruschetta, 45

Buffalo Chicken Wraps with Blue Cheese, 73

C

California Turkey Burger Sliders, 62

Cantaloupe
Balsamic-Drizzled Fruit and Cheese Bites, 23
Fruit Skewers with Creamy Marshmallow Dip, 93

Capers
Deviled Eggs, Three Ways, 51

Caramelized Onion, Mushroom, and Gouda Pinwheels, 77

Caramelized Shallot and Pine Nut Hummus, 34

Carrots
Hummus Veggie Pinwheels, 64
Veggie Wontons, 68–69

Cauliflower
Roasted Vegetable Kabobs, 27

Cheddar cheese
Mini Quiche Lorraine, 80–81
Mini Taco Bites, 72

Cheese boards, 56–57

Cheesecakes, Chocolate Chip Mini, 100–101

Cheeses. *See specific*

Cheese-Stuffed Chicken Meatballs Marinara, 70–71

Chef's Salad Skewers, 22

Chicken

Barbecue Chicken-Pineapple Bites, 54

Buffalo Chicken Wraps with Blue Cheese, 73

Cheese-Stuffed Chicken Meatballs Marinara, 70–71

Chicken Caesar Salad Cups, 55

Crispy Oven-Roasted Party Wings, 48–49

Mediterranean Marinated Chicken Skewers, 53

Peanut Chicken Endive Bites, 60–61

Chickpeas

Caramelized Shallot and Pine Nut Hummus, 34

Chives

Garlic-Ginger Portobello Mushrooms, 86–87

Chocolate

Chocolate Chip Mini Cheesecakes, 100–101

Double-Chocolate Brownie Bites, 94–95

S'mores Tarts, 105

Chunky Guacamole, 30

Cilantro

Avocado, Mango, and Pineapple Salsa, 32

Chunky Guacamole, 30

Fresh Tomato Salsa, 31

Spicy Black Bean Dip, 36–37

Cinnamon Sugar Pinwheels, 106

Cinnamon Swirl Mini Cupcakes, 98–99

Citrus-Garlic Marinated Olives, 16

Classic Party Meatballs, 65

Cocktail parties, 4–5

Cookies, Salted Peanut Butter, 96–97

Crab-Stuffed Mushrooms, 84–85

Cream cheese

Chocolate Chip Mini Cheesecakes, 100–101

Fruit Skewers with Creamy Marshmallow Dip, 93

Spinach Artichoke Dip, 39

Crispy Garlic Butter Smashed Potatoes, 89

Crispy Oven-Roasted Party Wings, 48–49

Cucumbers

Chef's Salad Skewers, 22

Greek Salad-Inspired Cucumber Bites, 26

Hummus Veggie Pinwheels, 64

Cupcakes, Cinnamon Swirl Mini, 98–99

D

Dairy-free

Avocado, Mango, and Pineapple Salsa, 32

Bacon-Wrapped Asparagus, 52

Barbecue Chicken-Pineapple Bites, 54

California Turkey Burger Sliders, 62

Caramelized Shallot and Pine Nut Hummus, 34

Chunky Guacamole, 30

Citrus-Garlic Marinated Olives, 16

Classic Party Meatballs, 65

Crispy Oven-Roasted Party Wings, 48–49

Deviled Eggs, Three Ways, 51

Fresh Tomato Salsa, 31

Garlic-Ginger Portobello Mushrooms, 86–87

Glazed Strawberry Tartlets, 104

Hummus Veggie Pinwheels, 64

Mediterranean Marinated Chicken Skewers, 53

Peanut Chicken Endive Bites, 60–61

Polenta with Lemony Tomato Bruschetta, 79

Quick and Easy Raspberry Refrigerator Jam, 40

Roasted Vegetable Kabobs, 27

Salmon Fritters, 88

Shrimp Satay with Peanut Dipping Sauce, 82–83

Spicy Black Bean Dip, 36–37

Sun-Dried Tomato-Garlic White Bean Dip, 35

Veggie Wontons, 68–69

Deviled Eggs, Three Ways, 51

Double-Chocolate Brownie Bites, 94–95

Drink pairings, 10–11

E

Eggs

Chef's Salad Skewers, 22

Chocolate Chip Mini Cheesecakes, 100–101

Deviled Eggs, Three Ways, 51

Mini Quiche Lorraine, 80–81

Salmon Fritters, 88

Endive Bites, Peanut
      Chicken, 60–61

Equipment, 7–8

Evening parties, 4–5, 10

F

Family friendly
      California Turkey Burger
            Sliders, 62
      Cheese-Stuffed
            Chicken Meatballs
            Marinara, 70–71
      Chicken Caesar Salad
            Cups, 55
      Chocolate Chip Mini
            Cheesecakes, 100–101
      Cinnamon Sugar
            Pinwheels, 106
      Cinnamon Swirl Mini
            Cupcakes, 98–99
      Classic Party Meatballs, 65
      Crispy Garlic Butter
            Smashed Potatoes, 89
      Crispy Oven-Roasted Party
            Wings, 48–49
      Deviled Eggs, Three
            Ways, 51
      Double-Chocolate Brownie
            Bites, 94–95
      Fruit Skewers with Creamy
            Marshmallow Dip, 93
      Glazed Strawberry
            Tartlets, 104
      Gourmet Parmesan-Herb
            Popcorn, 18
      Hummus Veggie
            Pinwheels, 64
      Mini Apple Pies with Crumb
            Topping, 102–103
      Miniature Baking
            Soda Biscuits for a
            Crowd, 46–47
      Mini Quiche Lorraine, 80–81

Mini Taco Bites, 72
Quick and Easy Raspberry
      Refrigerator Jam, 40
Raspberry Baked Brie en
      Croute, 76
Raspberry-Watermelon
      Smoothie Shooters, 92
Salted Peanut Butter
      Cookies, 96–97
Sheet Pan Party Pizza, 66–67
S'mores Tarts, 105
Spinach Artichoke Dip, 39

Feta cheese
      Balsamic-Drizzled Fruit and
            Cheese Bites, 23
      Fresh Basil Whipped
            Feta Dip, 33
      Greek Salad-Inspired
            Cucumber Bites, 26
      Marinated Feta with
            Rosemary and
            Orange, 25
      Stuffed Mini Sweet Peppers
            with Whipped Feta, 50

Fig, Gorgonzola, and Pear
      Tartlets, 78

5-ingredients
      Avocado, Mango, and
            Pineapple Salsa, 32
      Bacon-Wrapped
            Asparagus, 52
      Barbecue
            Chicken-Pineapple
            Bites, 54
      Buffalo Chicken Wraps with
            Blue Cheese, 73
      Caramelized Onion,
            Mushroom, and Gouda
            Pinwheels, 77
      Chicken Caesar Salad
            Cups, 55
      Chunky Guacamole, 30
      Cinnamon Sugar
            Pinwheels, 106

Citrus-Garlic Marinated
      Olives, 16
Crispy Garlic Butter
      Smashed Potatoes, 89
Crispy Oven-Roasted Party
      Wings, 48–49
Deviled Eggs, Three
      Ways, 51
Fig, Gorgonzola, and Pear
      Tartlets, 78
Fresh Basil Whipped
      Feta Dip, 33
Fresh Tomato Salsa, 31
Glazed Strawberry
      Tartlets, 104
Gourmet Parmesan-Herb
      Popcorn, 18
Greek Salad-Inspired
      Cucumber Bites, 26
Honey, Ham, and Brie Party
      Sandwiches, 63
Hummus Veggie
      Pinwheels, 64
Marinated Feta with
      Rosemary and
      Orange, 25
Marinated Mozzarella with
      Sun-Dried Tomatoes, 24
Miniature Baking
      Soda Biscuits for a
      Crowd, 46–47
Polenta with Lemony Tomato
      Bruschetta, 79
Quick and Easy Raspberry
      Refrigerator Jam, 40
Raspberry Baked Brie en
      Croute, 76
Raspberry-Watermelon
      Smoothie Shooters, 92
Rosemary-Garlic Whipped
      Ricotta Crostini with
      Prosciutto, 44
Rosemary-Thyme Parmesan
      Crisps, 20–21

5-ingredients (*continued*)

    S'mores Tarts, 105

    Stuffed Mini Sweet Peppers with Whipped Feta, 50

    Sweet and Spicy Roasted Nuts, 17

    Tomato Caprese Bruschetta, 45

Freezer staples, 6

Fresh Basil Whipped Feta Dip, 33

Fresh Tomato Salsa, 31

Fruit Skewers with Creamy Marshmallow Dip, 93

G

Garlic

    Caramelized Shallot and Pine Nut Hummus, 34

    Citrus-Garlic Marinated Olives, 16

    Crab-Stuffed Mushrooms, 84–85

    Crispy Garlic Butter Smashed Potatoes, 89

    Garlic-Ginger Portobello Mushrooms, 86–87

    Mediterranean Marinated Chicken Skewers, 53

    Peanut Chicken Endive Bites, 60–61

    Roasted Vegetable Kabobs, 27

    Rosemary-Garlic Whipped Ricotta Crostini with Prosciutto, 44

    Spicy Black Bean Dip, 36–37

    Sun-Dried Tomato-Garlic White Bean Dip, 35

    Veggie Wontons, 68–69

Ginger

    Garlic-Ginger Portobello Mushrooms, 86–87

    Peanut Chicken Endive Bites, 60–61

    Shrimp Satay with Peanut Dipping Sauce, 82–83

    Veggie Wontons, 68–69

Glazed Strawberry Tartlets, 104

Gluten-free

    Avocado, Mango, and Pineapple Salsa, 32

    Bacon-Wrapped Asparagus, 52

    Balsamic-Drizzled Fruit and Cheese Bites, 23

    Caramelized Shallot and Pine Nut Hummus, 34

    Chef's Salad Skewers, 22

    Chunky Guacamole, 30

    Citrus-Garlic Marinated Olives, 16

    Crispy Garlic Butter Smashed Potatoes, 89

    Deviled Eggs, Three Ways, 51

    Fresh Basil Whipped Feta Dip, 33

    Fresh Tomato Salsa, 31

    Fruit Skewers with Creamy Marshmallow Dip, 93

    Gourmet Parmesan-Herb Popcorn, 18

    Greek Salad-Inspired Cucumber Bites, 26

    Marinated Feta with Rosemary and Orange, 25

    Marinated Mozzarella with Sun-Dried Tomatoes, 24

    Mediterranean Marinated Chicken Skewers, 53

    Polenta with Lemony Tomato Bruschetta, 79

    Quick and Easy Raspberry Refrigerator Jam, 40

    Raspberry-Watermelon Smoothie Shooters, 92

    Roasted Vegetable Kabobs, 27

    Rosemary-Thyme Parmesan Crisps, 20–21

    Salmon Fritters, 88

    Spicy Black Bean Dip, 36–37

    Spinach Artichoke Dip, 39

    Stuffed Mini Sweet Peppers with Whipped Feta, 50

    Sun-Dried Tomato-Garlic White Bean Dip, 35

    Sweet and Spicy Roasted Nuts, 17

Good for leftovers

    Avocado, Mango, and Pineapple Salsa, 32

    Caramelized Shallot and Pine Nut Hummus, 34

    Cheese-Stuffed Chicken Meatballs Marinara, 70–71

    Chef's Salad Skewers, 22

    Chocolate Chip Mini Cheesecakes, 100–101

    Cinnamon Sugar Pinwheels, 106

    Cinnamon Swirl Mini Cupcakes, 98–99

    Citrus-Garlic Marinated Olives, 16

    Classic Party Meatballs, 65

    Double-Chocolate Brownie Bites, 94–95

    Fresh Tomato Salsa, 31

    Fruit Skewers with Creamy Marshmallow Dip, 93

    Marinated Mozzarella with Sun-Dried Tomatoes, 24

    Mini Quiche Lorraine, 80–81

    Quick and Easy Raspberry Refrigerator Jam, 40

Roasted Vegetable
Kabobs, 27

Salted Peanut Butter
Cookies, 96–97

Sheet Pan Party Pizza, 66–67

Shrimp Satay with Peanut
Dipping Sauce, 82–83

Spicy Black Bean Dip, 36–37

Spinach Artichoke Dip, 39

Sun-Dried Tomato-Garlic
White Bean Dip, 35

Gorgonzola, Fig, and Pear
Tartlets, 78

Gouda cheese
Balsamic-Drizzled Fruit and
Cheese Bites, 23

Caramelized Onion,
Mushroom, and Gouda
Pinwheels, 77

Crab-Stuffed
Mushrooms, 84–85

Gourmet Parmesan-Herb
Popcorn, 18

Graham crackers
S'mores Tarts, 105

Grapes
Fruit Skewers with Creamy
Marshmallow Dip, 93

Greek Salad-Inspired
Cucumber Bites, 26

H

Ham
Chef's Salad Skewers, 22

Honey, Ham, and Brie Party
Sandwiches, 63

Homemade Onion Dip, 38

Honey, Ham, and Brie Party
Sandwiches, 63

Hummus
Caramelized Shallot and
Pine Nut Hummus, 34

Hummus Veggie
Pinwheels, 64

I

Ingredient staples, 6–7

L

Lemons
Caramelized Shallot and
Pine Nut Hummus, 34

Citrus-Garlic Marinated
Olives, 16

Deviled Eggs, Three
Ways, 51

Mediterranean Marinated
Chicken Skewers, 53

Polenta with Lemony Tomato
Bruschetta, 79

Salmon Fritters, 88

Spicy Black Bean Dip, 36–37

Sun-Dried Tomato-Garlic
White Bean Dip, 35

Lettuce
Buffalo Chicken Wraps with
Blue Cheese, 73

Chef's Salad Skewers, 22

Chicken Caesar Salad
Cups, 55

Limes
Chunky Guacamole, 30

Fresh Tomato Salsa, 31

M

Make ahead
Avocado, Mango, and
Pineapple Salsa, 32

Balsamic-Drizzled Fruit and
Cheese Bites, 23

Barbecue
Chicken-Pineapple
Bites, 54

Buffalo Chicken Wraps
with Blue Cheese, 73

Caramelized Onion,
Mushroom, and Gouda
Pinwheels, 77

Caramelized Shallot and
Pine Nut Hummus, 34

Cheese-Stuffed
Chicken Meatballs
Marinara, 70–71

Chef's Salad Skewers, 22

Chocolate Chip Mini
Cheesecakes, 100–101

Cinnamon Sugar
Pinwheels, 106

Cinnamon Swirl Mini
Cupcakes, 98–99

Citrus-Garlic Marinated
Olives, 16

Classic Party Meatballs, 65

Crab-Stuffed
Mushrooms, 84–85

Crispy Garlic Butter
Smashed Potatoes, 89

Deviled Eggs, Three
Ways, 51

Double-Chocolate Brownie
Bites, 94–95

Fig, Gorgonzola, and Pear
Tartlets, 78

Fresh Basil Whipped
Feta Dip, 33

Fresh Tomato Salsa, 31

Fruit Skewers with Creamy
Marshmallow Dip, 93

Garlic-Ginger Portobello
Mushrooms, 86–87

Gourmet Parmesan-Herb
Popcorn, 18

Greek Salad-Inspired
Cucumber Bites, 26

Homemade Onion Dip, 38

Honey, Ham, and Brie Party
Sandwiches, 63

Hummus Veggie
Pinwheels, 64

Marinated Feta with
Rosemary and
Orange, 25

Marinated Mozzarella with
Sun-Dried Tomatoes, 24

Make ahead (*continued*)

Mediterranean Marinated Chicken Skewers, 53

Mini Apple Pies with Crumb Topping, 102–103

Miniature Baking Soda Biscuits for a Crowd, 46–47

Mini Quiche Lorraine, 80–81

Mini Taco Bites, 72

Peanut Chicken Endive Bites, 60–61

Quick and Easy Raspberry Refrigerator Jam, 40

Roasted Vegetable Kabobs, 27

Rosemary-Thyme Parmesan Crisps, 20–21

Salmon Fritters, 88

Salted Peanut Butter Cookies, 96–97

Shrimp Satay with Peanut Dipping Sauce, 82–83

Spicy Black Bean Dip, 36–37

Stuffed Mini Sweet Peppers with Whipped Feta, 50

Sun-Dried Tomato-Garlic White Bean Dip, 35

Sweet and Spicy Roasted Nuts, 17

Veggie Wontons, 68–69

Mango, Avocado, and Pineapple Salsa, 32

Marinara sauce

Cheese-Stuffed Chicken Meatballs Marinara, 70–71

Sheet Pan Party Pizza, 66–67

Marinated Feta with Rosemary and Orange, 25

Marinated Mozzarella with Sun-Dried Tomatoes, 24

Marshmallows and marshmallow creme

Cinnamon Swirl Mini Cupcakes, 98–99

Fruit Skewers with Creamy Marshmallow Dip, 93

S'mores Tarts, 105

Meatballs

Cheese-Stuffed Chicken Meatballs Marinara, 70–71

Classic Party Meatballs, 65

Mediterranean Marinated Chicken Skewers, 53

Melons

Balsamic-Drizzled Fruit and Cheese Bites, 23

Fruit Skewers with Creamy Marshmallow Dip, 93

Raspberry-Watermelon Smoothie Shooters, 92

Menu planning, 2–4, 12–13

Mini Apple Pies with Crumb Topping, 102–103

Miniature Baking Soda Biscuits for a Crowd, 46–47

Mini Quiche Lorraine, 80–81

Mini Taco Bites, 72

Mozzarella cheese

Balsamic-Drizzled Fruit and Cheese Bites, 23

Cheese-Stuffed Chicken Meatballs Marinara, 70–71

Marinated Mozzarella with Sun-Dried Tomatoes, 24

Sheet Pan Party Pizza, 66–67

Spinach Artichoke Dip, 39

Tomato Caprese Bruschetta, 45

Mushrooms

Caramelized Onion, Mushroom, and Gouda Pinwheels, 77

Crab-Stuffed Mushrooms, 84–85

Garlic-Ginger Portobello Mushrooms, 86–87

N

Nut-free

Avocado, Mango, and Pineapple Salsa, 32

Bacon-Wrapped Asparagus, 52

Balsamic-Drizzled Fruit and Cheese Bites, 23

Barbecue Chicken-Pineapple Bites, 54

Buffalo Chicken Wraps with Blue Cheese, 73

California Turkey Burger Sliders, 62

Caramelized Onion, Mushroom, and Gouda Pinwheels, 77

Cheese-Stuffed Chicken Meatballs Marinara, 70–71

Chef's Salad Skewers, 22

Chicken Caesar Salad Cups, 55

Chocolate Chip Mini Cheesecakes, 100–101

Chunky Guacamole, 30

Cinnamon Sugar Pinwheels, 106

Cinnamon Swirl Mini Cupcakes, 98–99

Citrus-Garlic Marinated Olives, 16

Classic Party Meatballs, 65

Crab-Stuffed Mushrooms, 84–85

Crispy Garlic Butter Smashed Potatoes, 89

Crispy Oven-Roasted Party Wings, 48–49

Deviled Eggs, Three Ways, 51

Double-Chocolate Brownie Bites, 94–95

Fig, Gorgonzola, and Pear Tartlets, 78

Fresh Tomato Salsa, 31

Fruit Skewers with Creamy Marshmallow Dip, 93

Garlic-Ginger Portobello Mushrooms, 86–87

Glazed Strawberry Tartlets, 104

Gourmet Parmesan-Herb Popcorn, 18

Greek Salad-Inspired Cucumber Bites, 26

Homemade Onion Dip, 38

Honey, Ham, and Brie Party Sandwiches, 63

Hummus Veggie Pinwheels, 64

Marinated Feta with Rosemary and Orange, 25

Marinated Mozzarella with Sun-Dried Tomatoes, 24

Mediterranean Marinated Chicken Skewers, 53

Mini Apple Pies with Crumb Topping, 102–103

Miniature Baking Soda Biscuits for a Crowd, 46–47

Mini Quiche Lorraine, 80–81

Mini Taco Bites, 72

Polenta with Lemony Tomato Bruschetta, 79

Quick and Easy Raspberry Refrigerator Jam, 40

Raspberry Baked Brie en Croute, 76

Raspberry-Watermelon Smoothie Shooters, 92

Roasted Vegetable Kabobs, 27

Rosemary-Garlic Whipped Ricotta Crostini with Prosciutto, 44

Rosemary-Thyme Parmesan Crisps, 20–21

Salmon Fritters, 88

Sheet Pan Party Pizza, 66–67

S'mores Tarts, 105

Spicy Black Bean Dip, 36–37

Spinach Artichoke Dip, 39

Stuffed Mini Sweet Peppers with Whipped Feta, 50

Sun-Dried Tomato-Garlic White Bean Dip, 35

Veggie Wontons, 68–69

Nuts

Peanut Chicken Endive Bites, 60–61

Sweet and Spicy Roasted Nuts, 17

O

Olives

Citrus-Garlic Marinated Olives, 16

Greek Salad-Inspired Cucumber Bites, 26

One pot

Avocado, Mango, and Pineapple Salsa, 32

Bacon-Wrapped Asparagus, 52

Buffalo Chicken Wraps with Blue Cheese, 73

Chunky Guacamole, 30

Citrus-Garlic Marinated Olives, 16

Fresh Basil Whipped Feta Dip, 33

Fresh Tomato Salsa, 31

Garlic-Ginger Portobello Mushrooms, 86–87

Gourmet Parmesan-Herb Popcorn, 18

Greek Salad-Inspired Cucumber Bites, 26

Honey, Ham, and Brie Party Sandwiches, 63

Hummus Veggie Pinwheels, 64

Marinated Feta with Rosemary and Orange, 25

Marinated Mozzarella with Sun-Dried Tomatoes, 24

Mini Taco Bites, 72

Quick and Easy Raspberry Refrigerator Jam, 40

Raspberry Baked Brie en Croute, 76

Raspberry-Watermelon Smoothie Shooters, 92

Rosemary-Thyme Parmesan Crisps, 20–21

Sheet Pan Party Pizza, 66–67

S'mores Tarts, 105

Spicy Black Bean Dip, 36–37

Stuffed Mini Sweet Peppers with Whipped Feta, 50

Sun-Dried Tomato-Garlic White Bean Dip, 35

Onions

Caramelized Onion, Mushroom, and Gouda Pinwheels, 77

Chunky Guacamole, 30

Crab-Stuffed Mushrooms, 84–85

Fresh Tomato Salsa, 31

Homemade Onion Dip, 38

Spicy Black Bean Dip, 36–37

Oranges

Citrus-Garlic Marinated Olives, 16

Oranges (*continued*)

Marinated Feta with Rosemary and Orange, 25

P

Pantry staples, 6–7

Parmesan cheese

Cheese-Stuffed Chicken Meatballs Marinara, 70–71

Chicken Caesar Salad Cups, 55

Gourmet Parmesan-Herb Popcorn, 18

Rosemary-Thyme Parmesan Crisps, 20–21

Spinach Artichoke Dip, 39

Party planning, 2–5, 12–13

Peanut butter

Salted Peanut Butter Cookies, 96–97

Shrimp Satay with Peanut Dipping Sauce, 82–83

Peanut Chicken Endive Bites, 60–61

Pear, Fig, and Gorgonzola Tartlets, 78

Pepperoni

Sheet Pan Party Pizza, 66–67

Peppers

Avocado, Mango, and Pineapple Salsa, 32

Crab-Stuffed Mushrooms, 84–85

Fresh Tomato Salsa, 31

Greek Salad-Inspired Cucumber Bites, 26

Hummus Veggie Pinwheels, 64

Roasted Vegetable Kabobs, 27

Spicy Black Bean Dip, 36–37

Stuffed Mini Sweet Peppers with Whipped Feta, 50

Pesto

Deviled Eggs, Three Ways, 51

Sheet Pan Party Pizza, 66–67

Tomato Caprese Bruschetta, 45

Piecrust

Mini Apple Pies with Crumb Topping, 102–103

Mini Quiche Lorraine, 80–81

Pies, Mini Apple, with Crumb Topping, 102–103

Pineapple

Avocado, Mango, and Pineapple Salsa, 32

Barbecue Chicken-Pineapple Bites, 54

Fruit Skewers with Creamy Marshmallow Dip, 93

Pine nuts

Caramelized Shallot and Pine Nut Hummus, 34

Fresh Basil Whipped Feta Dip, 33

Pizza, Sheet Pan Party, 66–67

Polenta with Lemony Tomato Bruschetta, 79

Popcorn

Gourmet Parmesan-Herb Popcorn, 18

gourmet variations, 18–19

Potatoes, Crispy Garlic Butter Smashed, 89

Prosciutto

Deviled Eggs, Three Ways, 51

Rosemary-Garlic Whipped Ricotta Crostini with Prosciutto, 44

Provolone cheese

Chef's Salad Skewers, 22

Puff pastry

Caramelized Onion, Mushroom, and Gouda Pinwheels, 77

Cinnamon Sugar Pinwheels, 106

Fig, Gorgonzola, and Pear Tartlets, 78

Raspberry Baked Brie en Croute, 76

Q

Quick and Easy Raspberry Refrigerator Jam, 40

R

Raspberry Baked Brie en Croute, 76

Raspberry-Watermelon Smoothie Shooters, 92

Ricotta cheese

Fresh Basil Whipped Feta Dip, 33

Rosemary-Garlic Whipped Ricotta Crostini with Prosciutto, 44

Stuffed Mini Sweet Peppers with Whipped Feta, 50

Roasted Vegetable Kabobs, 27

Rolls

California Turkey Burger Sliders, 62

Honey, Ham, and Brie Party Sandwiches, 63

Rosemary

Citrus-Garlic Marinated Olives, 16

Marinated Feta with Rosemary and Orange, 25

Rosemary-Garlic Whipped
    Ricotta Crostini with
    Prosciutto, 44
Rosemary-Thyme Parmesan
    Crisps, 20–21

S

Salmon Fritters, 88
Salted Peanut Butter
    Cookies, 96–97
Sausage
    Sheet Pan Party Pizza, 66–67
Scallions
    Mini Quiche Lorraine, 80–81
    Peanut Chicken Endive
        Bites, 60–61
    Roasted Vegetable
        Kabobs, 27
    Salmon Fritters, 88
    Veggie Wontons, 68–69
Serving essentials, 8–10
Shallot and Pine Nut Hummus,
    Caramelized, 34
Sheet Pan Party Pizza, 66–67
Shrimp Satay with Peanut
    Dipping Sauce, 82–83
S'mores Tarts, 105
Sour cream
    Homemade Onion Dip, 38
    Spinach Artichoke Dip, 39
Spicy Black Bean Dip, 36–37
Spinach
    California Turkey Burger
        Sliders, 62
    Spinach Artichoke Dip, 39
Stuffed Mini Sweet Peppers with
    Whipped Feta, 50
Sun-Dried Tomato-Garlic White
    Bean Dip, 35
Sweet and Spicy Roasted
    Nuts, 17

T

Tahini
    Caramelized Shallot and
        Pine Nut Hummus, 34
Tarts
    Glazed Strawberry
        Tartlets, 104
    S'mores Tarts, 105
30 minutes
    Avocado, Mango, and
        Pineapple Salsa, 32
    Bacon-Wrapped
        Asparagus, 52
    Balsamic-Drizzled Fruit and
        Cheese Bites, 23
    California Turkey Burger
        Sliders, 62
    Caramelized Shallot and
        Pine Nut Hummus, 34
    Chef's Salad Skewers, 22
    Chicken Caesar Salad
        Cups, 55
    Chunky Guacamole, 30
    Deviled Eggs, Three
        Ways, 51
    Double-Chocolate Brownie
        Bites, 94–95
    Fresh Basil Whipped
        Feta Dip, 33
    Fresh Tomato Salsa, 31
    Fruit Skewers with Creamy
        Marshmallow Dip, 93
    Garlic-Ginger Portobello
        Mushrooms, 86–87
    Glazed Strawberry
        Tartlets, 104
    Gourmet Parmesan-Herb
        Popcorn, 18
    Greek Salad-Inspired
        Cucumber Bites, 26
    Homemade Onion Dip, 38
    Honey, Ham, and Brie Party
        Sandwiches, 63
    Hummus Veggie
        Pinwheels, 64
    Marinated Feta with
        Rosemary and
        Orange, 25
    Marinated Mozzarella with
        Sun-Dried Tomatoes, 24
    Miniature Baking
        Soda Biscuits for a
        Crowd, 46–47
    Mini Taco Bites, 72
    Peanut Chicken Endive
        Bites, 60–61
    Polenta with Lemony Tomato
        Bruschetta, 79
    Raspberry-Watermelon
        Smoothie Shooters, 92
    Rosemary-Garlic Whipped
        Ricotta Crostini with
        Prosciutto, 44
    Salted Peanut Butter
        Cookies, 96–97
    S'mores Tarts, 105
    Spicy Black Bean Dip, 36–37
    Stuffed Mini Sweet Peppers
        with Whipped Feta, 50
    Sun-Dried Tomato-Garlic
        White Bean Dip, 35
    Sweet and Spicy Roasted
        Nuts, 17
    Tomato Caprese
        Bruschetta, 45
Tomatoes
    California Turkey Burger
        Sliders, 62
    Chef's Salad Skewers, 22
    Chunky Guacamole, 30
    Fresh Tomato Salsa, 31
    Mini Taco Bites, 72
    Polenta with Lemony Tomato
        Bruschetta, 79
    Roasted Vegetable
        Kabobs, 27

Tomatoes (*continued*)
    Sheet Pan Party Pizza, 66–67
    Spicy Black Bean Dip, 36–37
    Tomato Caprese
        Bruschetta, 45
Tomatoes, sun-dried
    Marinated Mozzarella with
        Sun-Dried Tomatoes, 24
    Sun-Dried Tomato-Garlic
        White Bean Dip, 35
Tools, 7–8
Tortillas
    Buffalo Chicken Wraps with
        Blue Cheese, 73
    Hummus Veggie
        Pinwheels, 64
Turkey
    California Turkey Burger
        Sliders, 62
    Chef's Salad Skewers, 22

V

Vegan
    Avocado, Mango, and
        Pineapple Salsa, 32
    Caramelized Shallot and
        Pine Nut Hummus, 34
    Chunky Guacamole, 30
    Citrus-Garlic Marinated
        Olives, 16
    Fresh Tomato Salsa, 31
    Garlic-Ginger Portobello
        Mushrooms, 86–87
    Glazed Strawberry
        Tartlets, 104
    Hummus Veggie
        Pinwheels, 64

Polenta with Lemony Tomato
    Bruschetta, 79
Quick and Easy Raspberry
    Refrigerator Jam, 40
Roasted Vegetable
    Kabobs, 27
Spicy Black Bean Dip, 36–37
Sun-Dried Tomato-Garlic
    White Bean Dip, 35
Veggie Wontons, 68–69
Vegetarian. *See also* Vegan
    Balsamic-Drizzled Fruit and
        Cheese Bites, 23
    Caramelized Onion,
        Mushroom, and Gouda
        Pinwheels, 77
    Chocolate Chip Mini
        Cheesecakes, 100–101
    Cinnamon Sugar
        Pinwheels, 106
    Cinnamon Swirl Mini
        Cupcakes, 98–99
    Crispy Garlic Butter
        Smashed Potatoes, 89
    Deviled Eggs, Three
        Ways, 51
    Double-Chocolate Brownie
        Bites, 94–95
    Fig, Gorgonzola, and Pear
        Tartlets, 78
    Fresh Basil Whipped
        Feta Dip, 33
    Fruit Skewers with Creamy
        Marshmallow Dip, 93
    Gourmet Parmesan-Herb
        Popcorn, 18

Greek Salad-Inspired
    Cucumber Bites, 26
Homemade Onion Dip, 38
Marinated Feta with
    Rosemary and
    Orange, 25
Marinated Mozzarella with
    Sun-Dried Tomatoes, 24
Mini Apple Pies with Crumb
    Topping, 102–103
Miniature Baking
    Soda Biscuits for a
    Crowd, 46–47
Raspberry Baked Brie en
    Croute, 76
Raspberry-Watermelon
    Smoothie Shooters, 92
Rosemary-Thyme Parmesan
    Crisps, 20–21
Salted Peanut Butter
    Cookies, 96–97
Spinach Artichoke Dip, 39
Stuffed Mini Sweet Peppers
    with Whipped Feta, 50
Sweet and Spicy Roasted
    Nuts, 17
Tomato Caprese
    Bruschetta, 45
Veggie Wontons, 68–69

W

Watermelon
    Fruit Skewers with Creamy
        Marshmallow Dip, 93
    Raspberry-Watermelon
        Smoothie Shooters, 92

ACKNOWLEDGMENTS

Every book project takes on a life of its own. It often takes the author away from other things because it takes time, dedication, and attention to write, test, retest, and finalize recipes. To that end, I have to thank my children, Will and Paige, for giving me the time and space to work on this cookbook and for lending their tummies to the recipe testing process. Your patience and love always make recipe development go well.

Thank you also to Gibran Graham for your tasting prowess and unwavering support, as well as for knowing when to tell me to walk away from my words. You're right. Coming back with fresh eyes always makes the writing better.

Thank you to all three for indulging me as I served only appetizers for dinner for so many nights during the recipe testing process. I promise to make full-size burgers on the grill soon.

Many of these recipes were inspired by parties I have held and been invited to over the years. Thanks, especially, to the Curious Cooks Cookbook Club for reminding me how much fun it is to enjoy a meal together and talk food. Thank

you also to my staff at the *Bangor Daily News*, past and present, for lending your taste buds to many cooking experiments over the years. And a warm remembrance to my college friends at Barnard and beyond for indulging my early cooking endeavors and dinner party dreams.

Thank you to my parents and siblings, Susan, Rick, Zach, and Haley, for always enthusiastically supporting my projects—even when it might seem like my schedule will split at the seams (it practically did this spring!). I always love to have you gather around my kitchen island and dig in.

As I write this, I am reminded of my late uncle Hugo and the magnificent spreads he'd prepare for holidays. It was around his and my Aunt Deb's table that I fell in love with antipasto. I wish he'd lived longer to see me take an interest in cooking, and so I could have learned from him.

Every cookbook I write has a soundtrack. This is no exception. A nod to the voices of the Great White Way—Broadway—for decades of show tunes that added spirit and levity to my recipe testing. Liza Minnelli, I couldn't have done this without you.

Food connects us with each other and with our past, present, and future. May this cookbook lead you to wonderful connections and tasty parties.

ABOUT THE AUTHOR

SARAH WALKER CARON is an award-winning food columnist, writer, and the voice behind the popular food blog *Sarah's Cucina Bella* (SarahsCucinaBella.com). She began writing about food in 2005 after her son, Will, was born. Since then, her work and writing have appeared in countless publications including *Fine Cooking*, *Bella Magazine*, *Yum for Kids*, BettyCrocker.com, and SheKnows.com. She is the author of *The Super Easy 5-Ingredient Cookbook* and *One-Pot Pasta*, co-author of *Grains as Mains: Modern Recipes Using Ancient Grains*, and also writes a monthly cooking column for *Bangor Metro* magazine. Named the 2015 Maine local columnist of the year by the Maine Press Association, Sarah is a graduate of Barnard College and lives in Maine with her two kids.